NEW ACCENTS

General editor: TERENCE HAWKES

# Telling Stories

# Telling Stories

## A theoretical analysis of narrative fiction

STEVEN COHAN AND LINDA M. SHIRES

London and New York

*First published in 1988 by*
*Routledge*
*11 New Fetter Lane, London EC4P 4EE*
*29 West 35th Street, New York NY 10001*

*Reprinted 1991, 1993*

*Photoset by Rowland Phototypesetting Ltd*
*Bury St Edmunds, Suffolk*
*Printed in England by Clays Ltd, St Ives plc*

*British Library Cataloguing in Publication Data*

*Cohan, Steven*
 *Telling stories: a theoretical analysis*
 *of narrative fiction.—(New accents).*
 *1. Cinema films. Narrative. Exposition.*
 *Critical studies.  2. Fiction. Narrative.*
 *Exposition – Critical studies*
 *I. Title   II. Shires, Linda M.*
 *III. Series*
 *791.43'09'0923*

 *ISBN 0-415-01386-0*
 *ISBN 0-415-01387-9 Pbk*

*Library of Congress Cataloging in Publication Data*

*Cohan, Steven.*
 *Telling stories.*
 *(New accents)*
 *Bibliography: p.*
 *Includes index.*
 *1. Narration (Rhetoric)   I. Shires, Linda M.,*
 *1950 –   . II. Title.   III. Series: New accents*
 *(Routledge (Firm))*
 *PN3383.N35C64   1988      808.3      88-15827*

 *ISBN 0-415-01386-0*
 *ISBN 0-415-01387-9 (pbk.)*

# Contents

| | | |
|---|---|---:|
| | *General editor's preface* | vii |
| | *Acknowledgments* | ix |
| *1* | *Theorizing language* | 1 |
| *2* | *Analyzing textuality* | 21 |
| *3* | *The structures of narrative: story* | 52 |
| *4* | *The structures of narrative: narration* | 83 |
| *5* | *Decoding texts: ideology, subjectivity, discourse* | 113 |
| *6* | *The subject of narrative* | 149 |
| | *Notes* | 176 |
| | *References* | 183 |
| | *Index of terms* | 191 |
| | *Index* | 193 |

# General editor's preface

It is easy to see that we are living in a time of rapid and radical social change. It is much less easy to grasp the fact that such change will inevitably affect the nature of those disciplines that both reflect our society and help to shape it.

Yet this is nowhere more apparent than in the central field of what may, in general terms, be called literary studies. Here, among large numbers of students at all levels of education, the erosion of the assumptions and presuppositions that support the literary disciplines in their conventional form has proved fundamental. Modes and categories inherited from the past no longer seem to fit the reality experienced by a new generation.

*New Accents* is intended as a positive response to the initiative offered by such a situation. Each volume in the series will seek to encourage rather than resist the process of change; to stretch rather than reinforce the boundaries that currently define literature and its academic study.

Some important areas of interest immediately present themselves. In various parts of the world, new methods of analysis have been developed whose conclusions reveal the limitations of the Anglo-American outlook we inherit. New concepts of literary forms and modes have been proposed; new notions of the nature of literature itself and of how it communicates are current; new views of literature's role in relation to society flourish. *New Accents* will aim to expound and comment upon the most notable of these.

In the broad field of the study of human communication, more and more emphasis has been placed upon the nature and function of the new electronic media. *New Accents* will try to identify and discuss the challenge these offer to our traditional modes of critical response.

The same interest in communication suggests that the series should also concern itself with those wider anthropological and sociological areas of investigation which have begun to involve scrutiny of the nature of art itself and of its relation to our whole way of life. And this will ultimately require attention to be focused on some of those activities which in our society have hitherto been excluded from the prestigious realms of Culture. The disturbing realignment of values involved and the disconcerting nature of the pressures that work to bring it about both constitute areas that *New Accents* will seek to explore.

Finally, as its title suggests, one aspect of *New Accents* will be firmly located in contemporary approaches to language, and a continuing concern of the series will be to examine the extent to which relevant branches of linguistic studies can illuminate specific literary areas. The volumes with this particular interest will nevertheless presume no prior technical knowledge on the part of their readers, and will aim to rehearse the linguistics appropriate to the matter in hand, rather than to embark on general theoretical matters.

Each volume in the series will attempt an objective exposition of significant developments in its field up to the present as well as an account of its author's own views of the matter. Each will culminate in an informative bibliography as a guide to further study. And, while each will be primarily concerned with matters relevant to its own specific interests, we can hope that a kind of conversation will be heard to develop between them; one whose accents may perhaps suggest the distinctive discourse of the future.

TERENCE HAWKES

# Acknowledgments

We want to thank our colleagues Jean Howard and Peter Mortenson for their helpful criticism of the first draft of chapters 1 and 2; Bennet Schaber and Tom Yingling for sharing their knowledge generously; Scott Busby of the Margaret Herrick Library, Academy of Motion Picture Arts and Sciences, for his assistance in locating film stills; Bryan Bates for his help in proofreading and preparing the index; Terence Hawkes and Sarah Pearsall for their careful attention to the manuscript; and especially Janice Price for her consistent interest and support.

Steven Cohan dedicates this book to Fay Albin Bolonik and Laura Jayne. Linda Shires dedicates this book to Sybil A. Ginsburg and U.C. Knoepflmacher.

Finally, we owe thanks and much more to each other for a collaboration in which we were not harmed by the other's faults but gained through each other's strengths.

We gratefully acknowledge permission to reprint:

*Cathy*, copyright 1986 Universal Press Syndicate. Reprinted with permission. All rights reserved.

"In a Station of the Metro" by Ezra Pound, *Personae*. Copyright 1926 by Ezra Pound. Reprinted by permission of New Directions Publishing Corporation. And from *Collected Shorter Poems*: reprinted by permission of Faber & Faber Ltd.

# Theorizing language

This book introduces a theoretical framework for studying narrative fiction. A *narrative* recounts a story, a series of events in a temporal sequence. Narratives require close study because stories structure the meanings by which a culture lives. Our culture depends upon numerous types of narrative: novels, short stories, films, television shows, myths, anecdotes, songs, music videos, comics, paintings, advertisements, essays, biographies, and news accounts. All tell a story. This definition of narrative provides the central premise of our book: the events making up a story are only available to us through a telling.

Today narratives tend to be in prose, although that has not always been the case by any means. Homer's epics, for example, are poetic narratives, and so are Samuel Taylor Coleridge's *The Rime of the Ancient Mariner* and Harry Chapin's song "Taxi": each tells a story in verse. The term "narrative" is often taken to exclude poetry simply because many poems are lyrics. Akin to song, a lyric is a monologue about feeling or a state of consciousness. Narratives give expression to feelings, but within the framework of a story and its telling. Whereas the lyric can be read as a private utterance, narrative must be taken as a public utterance; telling a story about characters' emotions mediates private experience to make it public. In this respect, narrative resembles drama but with one important difference: a play presents an action – Hamlet's duel with Laertes, say – directly, and a narrative does so indirectly, through the words which recount or describe the action. That narrative recounts and drama enacts persuades some critics to propose a strict definition of narrative as a purely verbal medium. Other critics, ourselves included, believe that the term "narrative" applies to the visual medium of storytelling as well. In a film, for instance, the camera recounts – because it records – events no less than a novel does. In both cases, the story is mediated by its telling – its medium of communication – so that the two are inseparable.

We can arrive at a working definition of narrative easily enough. The term *fiction*, on the other hand, poses much more of a problem. In its most common usage "fiction" means "not true." The typical disclaimer in films, which is also implicit in novels, that "any resemblance to persons living or dead is entirely coincidental," opposes fiction to fact and, thus, to truth or non-fiction. According to this view, the terms "fiction" and "non-fiction" designate two contrasting sets of expectations about language use: non-fictional language re-presents reality in a transcription, whereas fictional language represents it in a facsimile. Charles Dickens's *Bleak House* takes place in London, a real place in Britain, but is called a "novel," so one assumes as a matter of course that the book's language does not refer to anybody who actually lived or tell a story that actually happened. By contrast, when reading a biography of Charles Dickens or a history of London in the nineteenth century, one assumes just the opposite, that in this work of non-fiction language accurately recounts events as they happened.[1]

The seemingly obvious distinction between fiction and non-fiction is never quite so clear-cut. A few years ago, for example, the *Washington Post* ran a feature story about drug abuse by children. This story recounted the experience of one child in particular; following an accepted procedure in such types of stories, the author in the beginning of the article noted that she had changed the name of this child to protect his identity, and readers did not take the story to be any less factual. After this article won the Pulitzer Prize, it was discovered that the story's central figure was a composite portrait; the fictional name for the child did not refer to a real person after all. The writer was fired from the *Post* and the Pulitzer Prize committee rescinded the award, charging that the author had misrepresented the article. That disclosure changed the way the story was read. Once its status altered from being a case study to a composite – and thus fictional – portrait, so did its linguistic claim of being a re-presentation or transcription of an actual situation as opposed to being a representation or facsimile of one.

Like narrative, then, the term "fiction" also directs our attention to a story's medium of telling: language. Far from being a special or exceptional use of language, fiction, we propose, more accurately indicates how words mean than is normally thought. The relation between language and meaning, between words and what they refer to, is a highly complex one. To start explaining this complexity, we are going to look first at a type of language that does not rely on words at all and so does not immediately raise questions about referentiality: the language of driving. This example can help reorient the way we think about language; it can guide us to conceive of language as a powerful *system* of meaning-making. Then we shall look at some uses of language drawn from *Alice's Adventures in Wonderland* to show how verbal language works as a system similar to driving. With these examples we are laying the ground for discussing a theory of language and the production of meaning.

The language of driving uses shapes and colors more than words, but it is just as much of a language as English or Chinese. It consists of signs, colors, and shapes which have no material referent (and, in this respect, are fictive). Yet they communicate understandable meanings all the same. Such signs regulate traffic, describe conditions of the road, and so forth – as symbols. On traffic lights, for example, red specifically means "stop," green specifically means "go," and each color bears this symbolic value only within the context of the driving system.

Red and green signify these meanings on traffic lights because of *convention*. Conventions are cultural agreements about the relation of a sign and its meaning. In the traffic system the structuring of meaning through color has become so familiar that it is easy to forget "red" means the idea of stop but is not the same as that idea: red is a stand-in for the idea. As a symbol of "stop," furthermore, red is as arbitrary as the conventional practice of driving on the right-hand side of the road in

America as opposed to driving on the left-hand side in Britain. In other contexts, red can just as easily mean "blood" or "communism" or "Valentine's Day" or, for that matter, "cherry flavor." If our culture's conventions for traffic "grammar" differed, red could signify "go" just as easily as it now signifies "stop," and it could be placed at the bottom of traffic lights and green at the top. The conventionalized location of the two colors places them in an oppositional relation to each other: red means "stop" as the opposite of green, which means "go," and vice versa.

Syracuse, New York, offers an excellent example of the procedure by which the system of driving gives the colors red and green their distinct value as signs. An area of the city called Tipperary Hill with a large population of Irish descent has a traffic light which reverses the conventional locations of red and green colors (red is at the bottom and green at the top). Once this traffic light matched every other light in the city. But the neighborhood population kept shooting out the red light because it was over the green one. In this instance, the color symbolism of driving crossed that of political representation. Green traditionally signifies Ireland, while red signifies – on maps, say, or on army uniforms – Britain and the British Empire. Every time the city replaced the broken red light, someone in the neighborhood smashed it out again, until finally the city yielded and placed the green light at the top, the red light at the bottom. To a stranger in this neighborhood, that traffic light could pose a problem of interpretation because it does not follow the conventional alignment of color and location. In order to read the signal, one has to observe how other drivers read it, to see whether they follow the conventional meaning of the color alone or the color's unconventional location. In either case, interpretation is a public act; it involves knowing the system of conventions *and* negotiating the meaning of the sign with other drivers.

Red and green lights work as meaningful signs for the system of driving much as the words of any language do. Like driving, a verbal language such as English is also composed of signs that need interpretation. English does not use colors as its fundamental units of meaning, of course; it uses words, which do not function as consistently as colors do for driving and which therefore involve much more intricate acts of interpretation. But, like colors, words mean something only through convention and only as part of a communal system.

This last statement has considerable implications for understanding the relation between meaning and language, which we can begin to illustrate by looking at some examples of that relation's breaking down. Since its publication in 1865 Lewis Carroll's *Alice's Adventures in Wonderland* has fascinated people interested in language. The world of Wonderland, as typified by such odd characters as the Cheshire Cat and such odd situations as the Mad Hatter's tea party, seems strange, childlike, and unfamiliar to adult logic. But the real strangeness arises from the use of language in Wonderland. Alice's adventures are, in fact, *linguistic* misadventures. Not taking the linguistic system for granted, *Alice* offers vivid examples of the breaking down of language as a system of communication.

In Wonderland Alice has enormous difficulties understanding the creatures she meets, and they have just as much difficulty understanding her, because words seem to slip and slide into each other. For example, the Mouse begins to tell her "a long and a sad tale" (Carroll 1960: 35), but she hears "a long tail" and wonders why and how a *tail* can be sad. Further, when the Mouse contradicts something she has said by exclaiming, "I had *not*," Alice, thinking he has a "knot" in his tail, offers to undo it. Her gracious offer, however, actually offends the Mouse, who walks away saying, "You insult me by talking such nonsense!" (36). Her conversation with the mysterious Cheshire Cat also results in misunderstanding. The Cat first vanishes but then returns to ask Alice if she meant "fig" or "pig" when describing the transformation of the Duchess's child (64). Here the Cheshire Cat draws attention to a problem with words that compounds the earlier one. "Tail" and "tale" sound alike but are spelled differently. "Fig" and "pig," on the other hand, almost sound the same, just as they are almost spelled the same; what distinguishes one sound and spelling from the other is the initial consonant.

Similar words like "tail" and "tale," "not" and "knot," and even "fig" and "pig," mean something only so long as the form of one word can be distinguished from that of the other. The phonetic slippages which occur in these examples blur that difference to result in Alice's misunderstanding. Such slippage is not limited only to a word's phonetic form, since in Wonderland a word's meaning can even be transformed into its own negation. At Alice's trial before the Queen of Hearts, the King asks her what she knows. "Nothing," Alice replies, and the King instructs the jury, "That's very important." The White Rabbit, however, interrupts: "*Un*important, your Majesty means, of course." The King reverses his previous statement but is now unable to distinguish one word from the other: "'*Un*important, of course, I meant,' the King hastily said, and went on to himself in an undertone, 'important – unimportant – important – unimportant – important –' as if he were trying which word sounded best" (109). Not surprisingly, the jury is now very confused; some write down "important," some "unimportant." But no one seems more confused than the King himself. After reversing his original statement, he can no longer distinguish one word from the other; the meaning of either word depends upon an opposition between them which has disappeared. The presence of the negative prefix "un-" in one word and its absence in the other indicates this opposition, as the White Rabbit indirectly points out when he accents the prefix. In refusing to recognize the significance of that prefix – in making its importance unimportant, so to speak – the King collapses the crucial difference between the two words which allows them each to mean. And, once that happens, "important" ceases to exist as a concept of value for the King because it has been erased from his language.

These instances of misunderstanding all exemplify how an isolated word gains or loses meaning. Alice's misadventures with language also show how a word's meaning depends upon its placement in a sequence alongside other words. Slowly tumbling down the rabbit hole, she asks herself, "Do cats eat bats?" and "Do bats eat cats?" (19). For all the similarity of these questions, each asks something different. Depending upon the syntactic placement of the word "cats" or "bats" as the subject and not the object of her question, Alice could be asking about the eating habits of cats or about those of bats. Her confusion occurs because she cannot recognize this difference; since she "couldn't answer either question, it didn't matter much which way she put it" (19). The order does matter, of course, if she wants an answer.

The blurring of syntactic difference in Alice's question exposes as well the arbitrary relation between words and meanings. "Cat" and "bat" each refer to different types of animals. It makes all the difference in the world to the Mouse, for instance, that Alice is speaking of her cat, an animal he hates, and not her bat. All the same, even though cats and bats do not at all look alike, the words designating them resemble each other in sound and spelling to the point that Alice can exchange one for the other in her question.

The arbitrary attachment of words and referents becomes even more of an issue when the Cheshire Cat explains to Alice why he's mad:

> "To begin with," said the Cat, "a dog's not mad. You grant that?"
>
> "I suppose so," said Alice.
>
> "Well, then," the Cat went on, "you see a dog growls when it's angry, and wags its tail when it's pleased. Now *I* growl when I'm pleased, and wag my tail when I'm angry. Therefore I'm mad."
>
> "*I* call it purring, not growling," said Alice.
>
> "Call it what you like," said the Cat. (63–4)

This conversation between Alice and the Cat makes the relation between a word and its referent very problematic. What the Cat hears as "growling" is what Alice thinks of as "purring." "Call it what you like," the Cat responds. Although, as far as the Cat is concerned, the relation between a word and its referent is simply an arbitrary one, it does not necessarily follow that the word used is irrelevant. "Growling" and "purring" may refer to the same phenomenon – the same noise made by a cat – yet each word determines a different meaning for the noise. Calling it "purring" makes it appear as "normal" behavior for the animal, whereas calling it "growling" makes it appear as "mad" behavior.

In either case, to make sense of the noise, Alice and the Cat use a word that places it in a comparative framework. The Cat's word "growling" establishes a similarity between dogs and cats in order to point out the difference: if "growling" describes what a dog and the Cheshire Cat both do, then what is "normal" behavior for one animal is a sign of "madness" in the other. Alice's word "purring," on the other hand, places the noise in another kind of comparative framework, that of a dog's and cat's emotional states. "Purring," a word associated with cats, establishes the difference between the two animals in order to point out an underlying similarity: a dog wags its tail when happy and a cat purrs, just as a dog growls when angry and a cat switches its tail.

If not placed in such a comparative framework, a structure made possible by language, then the noise to which Alice and the Cat are both referring would simply remain a meaningless phenomenon, something indefinite because inarticulated. The Cat says, "Call it what you like," as if all possible words for this noise were the same, even a matter of personal choice. Yet call *what* what you like? Without a word, what does "it" refer to in the Cat's sentence? Language enables us, no less than it does Alice and the Cat, to distinguish the meaning of one sound from that of another. It is language which provides the structural framework that enables the noise to be conceived and thus perceived not as noise but as a distinct sound, growling *or* purring, and a meaningful sound at that, a sign of the Cat's madness or normality.

In still another instance of misunderstanding, Alice and the Mad Hatter talk to each other about time, but they each use the word "time" to refer to something different.

> Alice sighed wearily. "I think you might do something better with the time," she said, "than wasting it in asking riddles that have no answers."
>
> "If you knew Time as well as I do," said the Hatter, "you wouldn't talk about wasting *it*. It's *him*."
>
> "I don't know what you mean," said Alice.
>
> "Of course you don't!" the Hatter said, tossing his head contemptuously. "I dare say you never even spoke to Time!"
>
> "Perhaps not," Alice cautiously replied; "but I know I have to beat time when I learn music."
>
> "Ah! That accounts for it," said the Hatter. "He won't stand beating. Now, if you only kept on good terms with him, he'd do almost anything you liked with the clock." (69)

Because Alice and the Hatter each take literally a different figurative expression of time, neither understands what the other one means. To Alice time is a concept, so she uses the pronoun "it," whereas to the Hatter time is a person; he not only uses a different pronoun – the personal "he" – but also shows how that pronoun creates an entirely different conception of time.

Wonderland as a whole appears strange to Alice because the users of language there challenge the logic of common sense, which assumes that cats purr and that time is not a person. Alice thinks that sense is "common" because it transcends language; but, as both the Hatter and the Cheshire Cat demonstrate, sense is inseparable from language. What Alice calls the Cat's behavior determines its meaning and, moreover, assigns it a normative value. Likewise, her concept of time is not described by language but produced by it. For all her mastery of familiar linguistic patterns, the slipperiness of words like "tail" and "tale," "fig" and "pig," "important" and "unimportant," "cat" and "bat," "growl" and "purr" illustrate various ways in which words mean something only in relation to each other.


Ferdinand de Saussure, a Swiss professor of linguistics at the turn of this century, proposed a theory of language which, as developed further by a number of scholars in the last four decades, addresses the linguistic problems we have been raising in our discussion of *Alice*. Saussure outlined his theory of language in a series of lectures at the University of Geneva between 1906 and 1911; these were eventually written down by his students and published as *Course in General Linguistics* (1915). Saussure argued that language is a system of signs. "The linguistic sign," he explained, "unites, not a thing and a name, but a concept and a sound image" (Saussure 1966: 66). Placing special emphasis on the *sign* as the basic element of meaning and on *structures of differentiation* as the fundamental principle by which signs mean, Saussure explained that language is a system which structures relations between signs, and that these relations are what enable the articulation of a meaning. "Semiology," he proposed, "would show what constitutes signs, what laws govern them" (16). Towards this end, he distinguished between the language system itself, which he called "*langue*" (or "language"), and enunciations of a language, which he called "*parole*" (or "speech").

Semiotics, the study of sign systems of all kinds, has gone beyond Saussure's own interest in the relation between language and speech. A *sign* can thus be understood to combine a concept and a written or visual image as well as a spoken one, just as *parole* can extend beyond the spoken utterance. A more wide-ranging term for language use is "discourse," which includes any articulation of a sign system, written as well as spoken, non-verbal as well as verbal. The principle expressed through the distinction between *system* (*langue*) and *discourse* (*parole*) is thus not limited to verbal languages: it applies to any system of signs, such as games, film, painting, fashion, or driving.[2]

When Saussure showed that language operates as a sign system, he radically changed how one understands the relation between language and meaning. Language does not simply name things or ideas (though that is not to say that things and ideas do not have names). Language is not re-presentational, in the sense of transcribing meaning, but representational, in the sense of symbolizing it. The word "cat," for example, is not a name for a thing (the furry animal many of us keep as house pets but also the ferocious animals we can most commonly see in zoos and circuses). Rather, *cat* is a sign of that feline animal. This sign consists of a *signifier*, the particular combination of letters when written ("c-a-t"), or sound when spoken ("kat"), and a *signified*, the concept of "cat" which the signifier produces in our minds when we hear or read the word "cat." Likewise, on a traffic light, the red light itself is a sign, the color red is the signifier, and the command "stop" the signified. In short, all words are signs but not all signs are words.

The sign itself is the *relation* between signifier and signified; it holds them together as a unit of meaning. The relation between signifier and signified, which is the sign, looks like this:

|  | signified |  | feline animal |  | stop the car |
|---|---|---|---|---|---|
| SIGN } | —— | CAT } | —— | RED LIGHT } | —— |
|  | signifier |  | c-a-t/kat |  | red on top |

This chart is not another way of describing the word as a name (cat) for a thing (the feline animal). Once understood as signs, words can no longer be treated as transparent reproductions of reality; for upon close inspection it also becomes evident that the relation between the signifier and the signified is, Saussure stressed, an *arbitrary* one. There is nothing inherently feline in the word "cat" any more than there is anything inherently arresting in a red light.

As a consequence of appreciating both the difference between the signifier and signified and the arbitrary relationship between the two which constitutes the sign, one has to recognize that the signified is not the same as the *referent*, the object in reality. The signified of "cat" is a conceptualization of the animal, a mental construction. The feline animal does not appear in the sign – it is not there to be petted or to purr (which is why it must be signified).

That the signified is not the same as the referent is even more obvious when we use language to formulate ideas. Saussure concluded:

> Concepts are purely differential and defined not by their positive content but negatively by their relations with the other terms of the system. Their most precise characteristic is in being what the others are not. . . . Signs function, then, not through their intrinsic value but through their relative position. (Saussure 1966: 117–18)

For instance, when the King of Hearts decides that there is no difference between important and unimportant evidence, the sign *important* does not refer to anything outside of language but is actually a category of value constructed by language. You cannot find a material referent of the sign *important*, though you can indeed cite things you consider important. In doing that, however, you are still relating one sign to another, referring to other meanings produced in language, and participating in the system of comparison and contrast – of *differentiation* – that language makes possible. "In language," Saussure maintained as the fundamental axiom of semiotics, "there are only differences" (Saussure 1966: 120).

The differential field of a language system, Saussure went on to show, regulates the arbitrary relation of signifier and signified in terms of: *similarity*, the function of one sign when vertically compared to other signs; and *placement*, the position of one sign when horizontally combined with others. In learning a second language, for example, one studies much more than vocabulary, the system's repertoire of signs. Among other conventions of the language system, one has to learn verb conjugations – *I am, you are, it is*, and so forth – which establish patterns of subject–verb agreement. Actual use of English never reproduces this set of conjugations so schematically. Rather, the conjugation of a verb outlines its possible relations with a subject, which the language system makes available to its users. Such knowledge is necessary for recognizing the grammatical structure of a given utterance (*The cat is outside*, say) as a statement, a meaningful arrangement of signs and not a random combination. The statement *The cat is outside* organizes familiar signs – *cat, outside, is, the* – into a familiar pattern of subject–verb agreement, one which differs from other possible patterns of subject–verb agreement made available by the system, such as *I am outside* or *You are outside*.

Verb conjugations establish just one of the many *paradigms* which comprise a language system. "Those [signs] that have something in common are associated in the memory, resulting in groups marked by diverse relations" (Saussure 1966: 123). Paradigms are the sets of relationships, on the level of either the signifier or the signified, between a sign and all the other elements in the system. The motor-vehicle code outlines the paradigms of the driving system, just as the rules of chess outline the paradigms of the game, just as grammar books outline some of the paradigms of English. In addition to grammar, other common paradigms of English include rhymes (such as "fig" and "pig"), homonyms (words that sound the same, such as "tale" and "tail"), synonyms (words that mean the same, such as "tale" and "story"), and antonyms (words that mean the opposite, such as "growl" and "purr"). Each of these paradigms locates a sign within the language system by structuring a relation of similarity, on the level of signifier or signified, and this similarity helps to mark out the sign's identifiable difference from other signs. *Tale*, for instance, has the same phonetic signifier as *tail* but not the same signified; conversely, it has the same signified as *story* but not the same signifier. *Tale* is a distinct sign for this reason.

Saussure described paradigmatic associations as an effort of memory. His explanation does not fully consider how paradigms regulate the use of signs by enclosing them in a system. The paradigms of a language maintain its operation as a system by keeping its conventions stable and continually recognizable to users of the language – so stable and recognizable, in fact, that one is rarely conscious of the elaborate grid of similarity and difference which this system of paradigmatic marking constructs for language use. Phonetics, syntax, and semantics comprise major sets of paradigmatic relationships that classify groups of similar signs (nouns versus verbs, questions versus statements, animals versus fruits), and that differentiate one individual sign from another. A phonetic paradigm of the English language distinguishes the signifier "cat" from "bat" and from "dat," for example, by marking out the similarity in sound ("at") and the difference ("*k*at" as opposed to "*b*at" and "*d*at") which one needs in order to pronounce the word "cat." Similarly, a syntactic paradigm determines the function of the signifier "c-a-t" as a noun and not a verb in a sentence such as *The cat is outside*, and a semantic paradigm distinguishes this signifier from those of other animals ("b-a-t" and "d-o-g") and from other signifiers of feline creatures ("k-i-t-t-e-n" and "p-u-s-s" and even "W-h-i-s-k-e-r-s").

Semantic paradigms differentiate meaning on the level of the signified. To understand the meaning of *cat* is to recognize that it signifies something different from the concept of canine or rodent, and something different from the youthfulness signified by *kitten* as well. All the same, *cat* can signify many different things. It signifies either a class of small, tame feline animals (house pet) or large, wild ones (lion). It also signifies qualities associated with cats, such as stealthy movement, resilience, aloofness, and, in slang, a gossipy or promiscuous person. For that matter, to Alice *cat* signifies "pet," whereas to the mouse it signifies "enemy"! The many possible signifieds of *cat* suggest how easily language instigates a relay of signification to establish a network of interrelated signs that can, paradigmatically, substitute for each other: the signified of one sign (*cat*) easily becomes the signifier of another signified (pet, enemy, gossip, and so forth). This is essentially how connotation works, by relating a signifier to a variety of signifieds according to the semantic paradigms of the language system.

How does a language structure meaning to differentiate one signified from others in order to give a sign its precise meaning? In addition to paradigms, language also constructs meaning through *syntagms*, which position one sign along a chain of signs, as in a sentence. "In the syntagm a term acquires its value only because it stands in opposition to everything that precedes or follows it, or to both" (Saussure 1966: 123). Specific articulations of the system – the discourses we speak, hear, read, and write – consist of signs set in syntagmatic relation to each other. A sign thus acquires its specific meaning in part because of its paradigmatic location in the language system but in part because of its syntagmatic location in discourse too.

Whereas paradigms organize the vertical relations of similarity between one sign and others at the systemic level of language competence, syntagms organize the horizontal relations of contiguity between one sign and others at the discursive level of language performance. For example, the paradigms of chess determine a particular value for each playing piece, that the queen, say, is more significant than a pawn. But, in an actual game of chess, each piece also acquires its value according to its syntagmatic position on the board – what square it is on at any given time during the game, what pieces are next to it, what other pieces have been captured by the opponent, and so forth. As a sign of fashion, hair length functions in much the same way. Fashion operates according to a paradigm of conformity, a set of norms that determines what is in vogue and what is not. In the fifties and early sixties, long hair on men was considered unfashionable – anti-establishment, in fact – but only in comparison to short hair, which was the norm. In the late sixties and early seventies, however, the signs of fashion were reversed: long hair became a sign of fashion and, hence, the norm, whereas short hair signified old-fashioned, even reactionary in political and social values. In either case, what short or long hair signified as a sign of fashion depended on the length of a man's hair in syntagmatic relation to the way in which other men wore their hair at the same time.

A verbal language like English relies on the syntagmatic

arrangement of signs in even more intricate ways. Earlier we noted that *The cat is outside* is a meaningful statement because of its underlying paradigmatic structure. That statement is also meaningful because of the syntagmatic location of *The cat* in the particular sequence of words that make up the sentence. Moving *The cat* to the right of the verb *is* would change the syntagmatic structure to produce a question: *Is the cat outside?* Either sequence depends upon the exact order of words for its identity as a statement or a question, so its meaning is determined syntagmatically as well as paradigmatically.

Similarly, recall Alice's inability to tell the difference between the two questions "Do cats eat bats?" and "Do bats eat cats?" These two questions are indeed paradigmatically reversible insofar as each has the same underlying structure of auxiliary verb + subject + main verb + object. However, they are *not* syntagmatically reversible. In each version of her question, *cats* appears in a different syntagmatic relation to *bats*, so it signifies differently. In the first version *cats* is the subject, the agent of the action *eat*, while in the second version *cats* is the object, the goal or destination of that action.

Syntagms are most apparent in determining the identity of a sentence structure according to the actual sequential relation of its parts, but they also organize every aspect of discourse, from phrases of conversation to complete books. Syntagms place signs in a contiguous relation to each other, and these relations form the basis of complex meanings. When a noun is modified by an adjective (*black cat*), or a verb by an adverb (*purrs loudly*), the placement of one sign in relation to another syntagmatically determines a signified that neither word could bear singly. Likewise, relative and dependent clauses, participial phrases, parenthetical interjections, coordinate and subordinate sentence structures, and forms of figurative language arrange signs in a syntagmatic sequence. In each case, while paradigms make the underlying structure of the sequence possible, the value of a single sign is determined by the signs that surround it.

Although our examples so far may suggest otherwise, signs do not have to be directly adjacent to each other to be placed in syntagmatic relation. A pronoun, for instance, is a signifier which simply points elsewhere in the discourse for its signified, to a noun in close proximity that can serve as the pronoun's antecedent. When Alice uses "it" as a substitution for "time" in her conversation with the Mad Hatter, the pronoun *it* establishes a syntagmatic relation with the noun *time*. Alice and the Hatter each use the word "time" to refer to something different because the *words* they use keep pointing to other signifiers of time within two mutually exclusive syntagms, each producing a different meaning for time.

We have concentrated on the systemic structure of language, and have used as examples of non-verbal systems well-regulated languages such as driving. In doing so we have been following the parameters set forth by Saussure's theory of language. "Language," he claimed, "is a self-contained whole" (Saussure 1966: 9), "speech less speaking" (77). To define his object of study, he distinguished between a *synchronic* analysis of language as a static, timeless system, and a *diachronic* analysis more concerned with changes to the system that occur in speech over time. The primary importance of Saussure's synchronic model to contemporary studies of the sign lies in (1) his separation of the signifier and the signified; (2) his concentration on the differential basis of meaning; (3) and his analysis of the structural relations between signs. There are radical implications of this theory for thinking about the language of narrative, and we shall be returning to and building upon these three key points throughout.

But we must also acknowledge that Saussure's model has limitations for a full understanding of signs as cultural units of meaning. Saussure minimized discourse as a factor in the production and dissemination of signs. Signs mean something to and for someone, and they do so not in the abstract but in a discourse. All of our examples have illustrated both how language means systematically, and how language means only as it gets used. The tea party in particular shows what happens to the meaning of signs by virtue of their location in a particular instance of language use. Scholars who have critiqued Saussure's emphasis on a synchronically closed system of language agree that "meaning can belong only to a sign," but they also point out that "the sign cannot be separated from the social situation without relinquishing its nature as sign" (Vološinov 1986: 28, 37).[3]

It is tempting to conclude from Saussure's model that language is an unchanging, universal system governed by unalterable rules but, in actual practice, those rules do not always apply. For just as a driver might have to stop, even though the light is green, in order to avoid hitting a pedestrian, so too a writer might split an infinitive, rearranging the conventionally "correct" syntagmatic sequence of words, in order to forcefully make a point. A language system does not prescribe right and wrong uses for discourse so much as it establishes possible conditions of signification. In sum, a sign system does not "exist" materially as language in the way that discourse does. The system is merely an abstraction, a paradigmatic reconstruction of the principles governing actual language use and, thus, marking out possibilities of meaning for discourse.

The pairing of system/discourse, furthermore, is not hierarchical; discourse is not simply the concrete realization of a master system. Since discourse is the domain of actual language use, it stabilizes and conserves the system in which it operates, but it also continually revises the system to allow for new conditions by which meanings are produced. Revisions of grammar (such as the growing legitimacy of split infinitives), of spelling and punctuation (the different British and American styles), of pronunciation (regional dialects), of vocabulary (computer terminology), and of new ways of thinking about language and literature (the ideas informing this book), these are all changes in the language system of English that first occurred in discourse. Originating in usage, an alteration of the system becomes standardized – producing a genuine historical change of the system's paradigms – once users of the language consistently reproduce the alteration.

In the light of what we are saying about linguistic changes, it is also important to realize that neither a language system nor its discourse is ever singular, universal, and timeless. On the contrary, both are plural, cultural, and historical. We have spoken repeatedly of the language of driving as if the same system operates everywhere around the world in the same way, but that is far from the case. In California, for example, pedestrians have the right of way at intersections, so drivers routinely stop for anyone at a crosswalk; there, too, pedestrians can expect to be ticketed if they walk against a red light or cross in the middle of a street, and this practice encourages them to cross only at the marked intersections that give them the right of way. In New York, on the other hand, drivers do not automatically stop for pedestrians who step off the pavement, even at an intersection with a crosswalk; and pedestrians also routinely take the right of way, crossing against red lights when there is no oncoming traffic. While following the same system in many respects, the discourses of driving in these two states differ enough in practice to challenge and revise the competence of strangers.

What we are saying applies even more to a verbal language like English. As Alice's adventures demonstrate, while English may appear to be the same language to all its users, in practice just the opposite is true. Different English-speaking cultures use the language differently, as we have already indicated, so there are, in fact, many English languages, each regulated by a different version of the system and each further modified because of its interaction with other, non-verbal, cultural sign systems.

Moreover, in any given culture and historical time, individual speakers and writers of any one English language produce many different types of discourse. Spoken discourse, for example, varies according to the social situation: whether addressing friends, parents, teachers, strangers, clerks. Likewise, writing a letter, or a report, or a job application, or a civil service exam, or a literature paper depends upon one's ability as a user of English to produce a variety of discourses. In addition, writing can often turn out to be discursively plural, or heterogenic, even within the same piece of prose: when combining description, for instance, with exposition, or with argumentation. Each of these modes of writing comprises a different type of discourse, and combinations result in an even greater variety. Legal, medical, scientific, scholarly, business, technological, bureaucratic, and literary writing also use English differently, in that they follow different conventions of organization, style, documentation, vocabulary, and so constitute different discourses too. Using English, then, requires one's participation in a communal sign system which is historically specific, culturally located, and discursively varied. A sign system enables the production of meaning, but, in practice, discourse is where meanings actually get produced.

Saussure's attention to system (*langue*) over discourse (*parole*) – to language as "speech less speaking" – prevented him from considering that, while signs are regulated by a system, they are produced in and, more importantly, transformed by discourse. The limitations of Saussure's analysis have therefore required an extension of his theory in order to bring out its most radical implication: that in discourse a sign has the potential to *disrupt* as well as *facilitate* the passage of meaning because the relation of signifier to signified is unstable. While Saussure recognized the arbitrary and conventional features of the sign, he still treated a signifier as merely an expression of a signified. He did not fully consider the extent to which a signifier like the green light at Tipperary Hill in Syracuse produces a signified ("Irish") which functions as another signifier (of Ireland's historical political relation to Britain) in a relay of signification. A sign is thus not always bound by a system, as Saussure would have it, for a signifier can transgress the system.

Every use of language always positions a speaker (or writer, or listener, or reader) along a chain of signs. A sign, according to Charles S. Peirce, "addresses somebody, that is, creates in the mind of that person an equivalent sign, or perhaps a more developed sign" (Peirce 1955: 99).[4] The contemporary French philosopher Jacques Derrida puts this issue more extremely, perhaps, but very directly: "From the moment that there is meaning there are nothing but signs. *We think only in signs*" (Derrida 1976: 50).

Saussure did not acknowledge the complete dependency of meaning on signs. His privileging of speech over writing as the epitome of language use (*parole*) makes this clear. Despite what he explained about the sign, he still treated writing as a mere transcription of speech. "Language and writing," he stated, "are two distinct systems of signs; the second exists for the sole purpose of representing the first" (Saussure 1966: 23). Language, in this view, is constituted prior to rather than in writing, which simply performs the function of phonetic notation. As a result, Saussure attributed to the written sign a transparency of expression which he denied to the spoken sign. But elsewhere in the *Course in General Linguistics* Saussure also compared language to writing as "a system of signs that express ideas" (16). This kind of contradiction, Derrida argues in a very complex but important analysis, exposes the troubling status of writing in Saussure's theory of the sign.[5]

Far from transcribing speech, Derrida maintains, writing inscribes the absence which speech conceals or traces over, "the absence of the signatory, to say nothing of the absence of the referent. Writing is the name of these two absences" (Derrida 1976: 40–1). Writing signifies the difference from speech, the absence of an extra-linguistic ground, of a "transcendental signified which . . . would place a reassuring end to the reference from sign to sign" (49). In writing, "there is not a single signified that escapes, even if recaptured, the play of signifying references that constitute language. The advent of writing is the advent of this play" (7). Although discourse is in no way limited to writing, writing typifies how discourse presents us with a situation calling for interpretation, for stabilizing the play of signification. Unlike speech, writing foregrounds the constitution of discourse as a chain of references, not from sign to meaning, but from sign to sign.

Narrative, we said in opening this chapter, cannot be considered apart from language. The post-Saussurean theory of language as system and discourse, as structure and play, therefore demands a revision of traditional notions about narrative. To start with, this theory calls for rigorous attention to narrative as a set of signs. It requires a method of textual analysis responsive to both the structuring operation of a sign system and the instability of signs in discourse.

# 2

# Analyzing textuality

The theory of language presented in chapter 1 argues against the commonplace assumption that meaning is a "content" translated into words. Language structures possibilities of meaning because it structures relations of difference (the basis of the sign), of similarity (the basis of paradigms), of placement (the basis of syntagms). Analysis of a text therefore requires breaking it into segments in order to expose the paradigmatic, syntagmatic, and semiotic markings that organize relations of similarity, placement, or difference. Such markings inscribe the text with various stresses, making it appear "stress-full" in several ways. The markings emphasize certain signifiers over others; they put pressure on the seemingly "natural" and closed relation between signifiers and signifieds; and they can strain understanding, causing a reader to ask, what does this word, phrase, sentence mean? These markings of stress (emphasis, pressure, and strain) are signs of *textuality*: language conceived of as "productivity, the production of a multiplicity of signifying effects" (Young 1981: 8).

The purpose of this chapter is to conceptualize relations between words so that the textuality of language can be analyzed. The question we are addressing is not what a given text means, but how it is that a text can mean something. Indeed, we want to expand upon this question to consider how it is that a text can have the potential for multiple meanings, not just one single meaning, but also not just any meaning. In this chapter we are, therefore, continuing the discussion of language begun in the first chapter by explaining how textual analysis helps to expose the semiotic conditions that make meanings possible.

Since the theory of language we presented in chapter 1 reconceives the relation between language and meaning, it demands, as well, a reconsideration of the traditional practices of reading language critically. Traditional literary criticism pays close attention to language, to be sure, but it justifies this attention by treating literature as a special use of language which requires readers to have what Jonathan Culler has called, in an analogy to linguistic competence, *literary competence*: "a set of conventions for reading texts [as literature]" (Culler 1975: 118). As with all uses of language, literary competence is not intuitive but learned. To be a competent reader of literary discourse, one must acquire knowledge of formal conventions, such as tropes and meter, so as to recognize the literary features of, say, a poem. More importantly, one must also acquire knowledge of the conventions that can be used to analyze and interpret these features.

According to Culler, three basic conventions of analysis inform traditional literary competence. These are: (1) the convention of significance, that a work of literature is "expressing a significant attitude to some problem concerning man and/or his relation to the universe"; (2) the convention of metaphorical coherence, that the work's figural devices (such as metaphor itself, but also alliteration, rhyme, and so forth) produce coherence on the levels of both signifier and signified; (3) the convention of thematic unity, that the linguistic features of the work, identified through the method of analysis laid out by the second convention, provide it with a unifying formal structure that reinforces the determinate meaning expected because of the first convention (Culler 1975: 115).

The conventions of literary competence reproduce a fundamental and often unquestioned assumption motivating traditional understanding of literature: that essential linguistic qualities distinguish literary from non-literary discourse, and that from these features discerning readers, trained in literature, can recover a timeless meaning placed in a work by its author. This assumption, however, is just another convention of literary competence, for what we said in chapter 1 about fictive and non-fictive language applies to the traditional distinction between literary and non-literary language too. Literature itself is not a specialized use of language which absolutely distinguishes one class of discourse (the literary: aesthetically self-contained objects with a concealed meaning expressing human values) from another (the non-literary: pragmatically motivated communications of transparent meaning). Rather, literature is actually a set of culturally and historically defined conventions for reading texts in one way as opposed to another. "In this sense," Terry Eagleton comments, "one can think of literature less as some inherent quality or set of qualities displayed by certain kinds of writing all the way from *Beowulf* to Virginia Woolf, than as a number of ways in which people *relate themselves* to writing" (Eagleton 1983: 9).[1]

Being a set of conventions for reading, literary competence is a social (and socializing) practice, reproduced through various institutions (e.g. school, the media, book publishing and reviewing, sponsorship of the arts, and so forth) which teach or, more implicitly, reproduce conventions of reading and which certify the identity and value of some works as literature. What constitutes a reader's literary competence is thus subject to change, since, at different historical moments and in different cultures, what people read and value, and how they do so, differs. As Eagleton puts it:

The fact that we always interpret literary works to some extent in the light of our own concerns – indeed that in one sense of "our own concerns" we are incapable of doing anything else – might be one reason why certain works of literature seem to retain their value across the centuries. It may be, of course, that we still share many preoccupations with the work itself; but it may also be that people have not actually been valuing the "same" work at all, even though they may think they have. "Our" Homer is not identical with the Homer of the Middle Ages, nor "our" Shakespeare with that of his contemporaries; it is rather that different historical periods have constructed a "different" Homer and Shakespeare for their own purposes, and found in these texts elements to value or devalue, though not necessarily the same ones. All literary works, in other words, are "rewritten," if only unconsciously, by the societies which read them; indeed there is no reading of a work which is not also a "re-writing." No work, and no current evaluation of it, can simply be extended to new groups of people without being changed, perhaps almost unrecognizably, in the process; and this is one reason why what counts as literature is a notably unstable affair. (Eagleton 1983: 12)

The conventions of reading texts as "literature" vary historically and culturally, though they are institutionalized as universal givens about the "essential" qualities of literary works much in the way that the conventions of driving are institutionalized: codified, taught, and so legitimatized as uncontestable rules governing the paradigms of the system.

It is important to recognize that a reader's literary competence is like his or her competence in other semiotic practices (driving, games, fashion), for, while literary conventions are, at times, valuable tools of analysis, they are not neutral tools. Any convention that performs a function presupposes the conditions that warrant the function. Literary conventions are no exception. The expectations of a work's universal significance, metaphorical coherence, and thematic unity define an agenda for reading which has political and social implications in what it excludes as well as includes. Assuming that a work can be reduced to a theme about "man and/or his relation to the universe" privileges historical and cultural criteria of what counts as significant by treating these values as if they were universal. In its universalizing notion of "man," moreover, this expectation about literature suppresses issues of culture, race, class, and gender that question the western, white, patriarchal, and bourgeois conception of "man" as a synonym for the "human." Similarly, to look for metaphorical coherence as formal evidence of a work's thematic unity is to disregard additional linguistic activity and alternative meanings which challenge the belief that literature is a self-contained, aesthetically unified object.

In later chapters we shall return to the politics of meaning; our immediate concern is how language marks a range of potential meanings. The language of a text can cooperate with literary conventions to a large extent. But language, we are arguing, also resists the agenda which literary conventions set for analysis. To find unity and coherence in a text according to the conventions of reading taught as literary competence, one must somehow reconcile difference through similarity. Such reconciliation only occurs by fixing what language unfixes and makes unstable, namely, the semiotic differentiation that comprises textuality as a relay of signifiers. Literary conventions accomplish this fixing by leading a reader to a determinate and unifying meaning, a final signified. All the same, language itself disrupts the coherence and unity which seemingly confirm but actually motivate the stabilizing conventions governing the way in which texts have been traditionally read as "literature."

To be more responsive to the disrupting movements of a text, readers need what we can call "textual competence," the learned ability to negotiate the slippages of language. Whereas literary analysis subordinates a work's signifiers to a final signified, textual analysis, on the other hand, concentrates on language as a field of signifiers which multiplies possibilities of meaning. As Roland Barthes explains,

> textual analysis impugns the idea of a final signified. The work does not stop, does not close. It is henceforth less a question of explaining or even describing, than of entering into the play of the signifiers; of enumerating them, perhaps (if the text allows), but not hierarchising them. Textual analysis is pluralist. (Barthes 1981: 43)

In his many essays and books on texuality, Barthes defines *text* in opposition to *work*. As traditionally used, *work* designates writing read as a completed product that conveys a preexistent (and persistent) intended meaning. With its object of inquiry defined in this way, Barthes pointed out, "[traditional] criticism seeks in general to discover the meaning of the work, a meaning which is more or less hidden and which is assigned to diverse levels, depending on the critic" (Barthes 1981: 43). So understood to be repeating the "hidden" intentions of the author, a *work* places its meaning outside of the play of signifiers that is language.

In contrast to the *work*, the *text*, according to Barthes, is "a methodological field . . . the work can be held in the hand, the text is held in language, only exists in the movement of a discourse." A *text* is an ongoing "production" rather than a finished product because "its field is that of the signifier," which generates, for a reader, "a serial movement of disconnections, overlappings, variations." Since it defers ever reaching or closing upon a final signified, the text is "restored to language; like language, it is structured but off-centred, without closure." And as a result of its "infinite *deferment* of the signified" [our italics] the *text* is "plural." Its plurality is "irreducible" to a single final meaning. Being a *text*ure, a "weave of signifiers," the plurality of a *text* amounts "not [to] a co-existence of meanings but [to] a passage, an overcrossing; thus it answers not to an interpretation, even a liberal one, but to an explosion, a dissemination" – that is, to the movement of words as signifiers exceeding a final signified (Barthes 1977: 157–9).

Textual analysis is an activity of play in several senses: reading is a performance, like playing a musical score; it responds to the play of meanings in language; and it is a source of pleasure, play as opposed to work. In reconceiving the "work" as a "text," one must remember that the term "text" is itself a stress-full signifier caught up in the play of language. As Robert Young cautions,

> the word enacts its own meanings, a wandering of significa-
> tion which is, precisely, text. . . . the word never reaches its
> point of limit, but wanders and redoubles upon itself in its
> meanings of text as a critical value, text as a replacement for
> the work, text as pleasure, text as a discursive unit, textuality
> as a tissue of signifying practices, text as the (critical) activity
> which textualises and analyses these movements. (Young
> 1981: 31–2)

We can illustrate some of the linguistic movement that characterizes textuality by analyzing a short piece of discourse first as a "work" and then as a "text."

*In a Station of the Metro*
The apparition of these faces in the crowd;
Petals on a wet, black bough.

A traditional analysis of this poem by Ezra Pound follows the three conventions of literary analysis as outlined by Culler.

Assuming that this work expresses a significant statement about human nature, a reader uses her or his literary competence to recognize the poetic conventions that foreground certain linguistic features; then the reader organizes these properties into a coherent pattern as evidence of the work's thematic unity. From this perspective, two figural devices in particular stand out in relation to the poem as a whole. The poem uses *synecdoche*, a rhetorical device in which a part of something or someone signifies the whole, when referring to people in terms of their faces and to flowers in terms of their petals; and it brings the two synecdoches together in a *metaphor*, a rhetorical device which establishes the similarity of two unlike things by treating them as identical: faces in the crowd = petals on a bough. Several additional "poetic" features focus attention upon the metaphor. That the poem is lineated, with lines set apart from each other on the page, stresses the words that end each line, "crowd" and "bough," and an internal rhyme (the repetition of an "ow" sound in each) also emphasizes the pairing of these two words. Furthermore, although this poem lacks metric regularity (a repeated pattern of accented/unaccented syllables), it still relies on *cadence*, or recurrence of metric emphases: the phrase "black bough" consists of two stressed monosyllabic words in a row. Finally, *alliteration*, the repetition of consonant sounds usually at the beginning of words, also emphasizes that final phrase. In sum, the various stresses on "crowd" and, especially, "bough" mark these two words to reinforce a final signified of the metaphor's equation of unlike things. These "poetic" features, then, unify the whole poem around the metaphor as a thematic statement: even underground in a subway station, inherently natural qualities in people shine forth through their faces.

This analysis draws upon the conventions of universal significance, metaphorical coherence, and thematic unity to recover a meaning which is seemingly present in the poem's language, awaiting discovery by competent readers. The theory of textuality, however, argues that significance, coherence, and unity are not formal properties of language but conventions of reading language in a certain way, i.e. as literature: "the poem [should] be thought of as an utterance that has meaning only with respect to a system of conventions which the reader has assimilated. If other conventions were operative its range of potential meanings would be different" (Culler 1975: 116). Put another way, we can see the poem linguistically reproducing its metaphoric content only so long as we let the metaphor determine what we do and do not look for in the language. When the poem is looked at differently – that is, as a *text* – the metaphor turns out to be a linguistic pressure-point which disrupts the coherence it attempts to achieve.

Rather than organizing the poem into a unified and coherent whole, the metaphor actually opens up, as it were, a hole in the text. While the metaphor calls attention to a similarity of seeming opposites (faces of people/petals of flowers), it does not identify what, specifically, makes them equal. That the metaphor does *not* lead to a single determinate meaning establishes a gap between the text's signifiers and a final signified. This gap invites readers to interpret the metaphor; but the gap also places stress (pressure) on the metaphor, which is only another signifier. Unless we treat the metaphor itself as a signifier, we cannot interpret it but can only paraphrase the comparison it already describes.

Literary conventions may encourage readers to expect the metaphor to unify the poem, but the metaphor cannot contain all the linguistic activity of the text. Notice, in particular, the punctuation in the second line: the comma divides the line in half, sliding "wet" a bit closer to "petals" implicitly to modify it. And once "wet" is broken loose of "black bough" it may also modify "faces," which is metaphorically identified with "petals," and it can, certainly, modify the Metro station, damp because it is underground. That the Metro station is probably dark for the same reason it is damp also dislocates "black" from "bough." Once this happens there is no stopping "black." It points forward to "bough," up the page to "station" in the title, and backward to "petals" and even to "faces."

Since "wet" and "black" have the potential to signify all the nouns of the poem, the two adjectives imply a set of relations between the nouns based on metonymy. *Metonymy* is a rhetorical device in which one term, through actual proximity or widespread association, has become closely enough identified with another term to signify it; "Metro station" is a metonymy of

Paris, just as "tube" is a metonymy of London. In this text we have discovered a structuring operation based not on resemblance, the principle of metaphor, but on contiguity, the principle of metonymy. Though placed directly next to "bough," "wet, black" metonymically signifies "Metro station" because of association, and "petals" because of location (on the bough), and "faces" because of location (in the Metro) and association (the equivalence with "petals").

As a result of this metonymic realignment, a reader begins to confront oppositions that the metaphor has concealed. Everything that the faces in the crowded Metro station signify (e.g. city, modern, human, machine, underground, darkness, dankness, movement) necessarily implies its opposite (not nature, not timeless, not things, not organic, not above ground, not sunlit, not fresh, not peaceful). Sustained in turn by the other side of the metaphoric equation, the petals on the bough, these oppositions delineate the boundaries of meaning for the text, what it places at issue: whether "the apparition" is an impression of the naturalness of these modern urban faces, or whether it is an impression of unnaturalness.

In order to forge an equivalence of such binary oppositions, the metaphor can only join them together by privileging similarity and denying difference. The metaphor treats "faces" (and its set of signifieds) and "petals" (and its set of signifieds) as if they were in a *paradigmatic* relation to each other. With one side of the polarity made equivalent to the other, one set of signifiers and signifieds can be substituted for the other, and the metaphor can then reconcile, even collapse, the binary oppositions that "faces" and "petals" generate as a pair of differential signs. The text, however, sets "faces" and "petals" in a *syntagmatic* relation to each other. Since these two terms occupy different places in the metaphor's structuring of equivalence, the oppositions exceed the metaphor: if each side of the metaphoric equation were indeed identical, one could be substituted for the other without affecting the text's syntagmatic structure, but this is not the case, since the reversal of "these faces in the crowd" and "petals on a wet, black bough" in lines 1 and 2 would produce another text. The text's language jams the apparently straightforward equation drawn by the metaphor. So the metaphor must be analyzed as a response to the oppositions which, circulating through the text, establish the conditions of its possible meanings.


Our objective in analyzing the poem as a text was not to recover a meaning but, rather, to uncover the range of possible (even competing) meanings inscribed in its language. To do so, we conceived of the poem as a text, segmenting it by applying the three fundamental principles of linguistic organization that we discussed in the first chapter: (1) similarity, (2) placement, (3) difference. Using the first principle we segmented the text to find perceived resemblances, noticing the metaphoric equation of "faces" and "petals." Using the second principle we segmented the text to find perceived contiguities, noticing the placement of "wet, black" in metonymic relation to "petals," "faces," and "Metro station." Finally, using the third principle, we segmented the text to find perceived binary oppositions: nature/city, fresh/stale, light/dark, etc.

We could treat this poem as an example of textuality, moreover, not because the poem is a special instance of poetry or because poetry itself is a special use of language, but because textuality characterizes all uses of language. To be sure, our textual analysis relied extensively on rhetorical figures such as metaphor and metonymy, which have traditionally been considered the special linguistic province of poetry, literary as opposed to non-literary discourse. Metaphor and metonymy, however, appear so repeatedly in all uses of language that one often gives them little notice. When speaking of a "growling stomach" or "the social fabric," one is using a metaphor; likewise, when speaking of the American presidency as "the White House" or the British royal family as "Buckingham Palace," one is using a metonymy.

Such commonplace examples, though, do not indicate the complexity of metaphor and metonymy in so-called non-literary and non-fictive discourse. The following excerpt from Lewis Thomas's memoir *The Youngest Science* relies on both metaphor and metonymy in ways that may not be immediately obvious – and in ways that do not work in concert.

One thing the nurses do is to hold the place together. It is an astonishment, which every patient feels from time to time, observing the affairs of a large, complex hospital from the vantage point of his bed, that the whole institution doesn't fly to pieces. A hospital operates by the constant interplay of powerful forces pulling away at each other in different directions, each force essential for getting necessary things done, but always at odds with each other. The intern staff is an almost irresistible force in itself, learning medicine by doing medicine, assuming all the responsibility within reach, pushing against an immovable attending and administrative staff, and frequently at odds with the nurses. The attending physicians are individual entrepreneurs trying to run small cottage industries at each bedside. The diagnostic laboratories are feudal fiefdoms, prospering from the insatiable demands for their services from the interns and residents. The medical students are all over the place, learning as best they can and complaining that they are not, as they believe they should be, at the epicenter of everyone's concern. Each individual worker in the place, from the chiefs of surgery to the dieticians to the ward maids, porters, and elevator operators, lives and works in the conviction that the whole apparatus would come to a standstill without his or her individual contribution, and in one sense or another each of them is right.

My discovery, as a patient first on the medical service and later in surgery, is that the institution is held together, *glued* together, enabled to function as an organism, by the nurses and by nobody else. (Thomas 1983: 66–7)

The point of this passage may seem straightforward enough not to require any analysis at all: nurses are metaphorically compared to glue, they unify the various parts of a hospital so that it can function as a whole. But two other metaphoric comparisons raise a question about the "whole" identity of the hospital as an institution: is it an "apparatus," the parts of which must be glued together, or an "organism" which is naturally whole?

According to this passage, a hospital is a field of natural energy rather like the sun, and it is also an industrial machine. In the second and third sentences nursing is metaphorically equated with a center of gravity, the hospital equated with centripetal force, the various working units equated with forces of power, the institution equated with centrifugal force. This metaphor of nature is repeated in the fourth sentence's description of the intern staff as an "irresistible" force of centripetal energy, and it reappears later in "epicenter" (the geological signifier of the medical students' self-interest), and in "come to a standstill" (a signifier of stasis that repeats the metaphor of natural energy through opposition). A metaphor of industry and economics, by contrast, proposes an alternative depiction of the hospital as something manufactured, an "apparatus." The hospital is metaphorically equated with a machine in the third sentence (it "operates"), and in the second half of the first paragraph physicians are compared to "entrepreneurs" running "small cottage industries," and the laboratories to "feudal" – and "prospering" – "fiefdoms." In closing, the passage returns to the originating metaphor of nurses gluing the place together and enabling it to "function as an organism." The last sentence thus replaces the two previous signifiers of the hospital – "the whole institution" and "the whole apparatus" – with "organism" in order to privilege the natural metaphor over the industrial one.

Yet, when joined in a syntactic unit, that verb "function" and noun "organism" sustain the binary opposition of industry and nature which the entire passage repeats. The metaphors organize a degree of similarity (a whole) out of difference ("forces . . . always at odds with each other"). The description of the heterogeneous "affairs of a large complex hospital" belies any similarity, for it breaks down the hospital into component and conflicting parts: not only "every patient" and "vantage point of his bed," but also the nurses, interns, administrative staff, attending physicians, lab technicians, medical students, chiefs of surgery, dieticians, ward maids, porters, elevator operators. Each of these is a metonymy of the hospital; and they all suggest that the totality of the hospital consists of differing workers united in a common enterprise only by virtue of their contiguous relation to each other in one location. That these various parts exceed either of the metaphoric wholes becomes evident when one notices that the metaphors can treat the hospital as a whole only by excluding some of its parts. The natural metaphor includes the nurses, interns, and students but excludes the attending physicians and diagnostic laboratories, and the industrial metaphor does just the reverse.

As a result, neither the natural nor the industrial metaphor can resolve an opposition which signifies the hospital through its metonymies: those medical workers motivated by humanitarian values and joined together in the natural metaphor versus those motivated by economic values and joined together in the industrial metaphor. So read as a linguistic structure arranged by metonymy as well as metaphor, the passage can now be analyzed as a production of competing meanings: "astonishment" over the hospital's heterogeneity, as depicted through the metonymies, and "conviction" that it is unified, as depicted through the metaphors.

In analyzing this passage we have assumed that metaphor and metonymy are much more than figures of speech which merely dress up meanings. Rather, they are fundamental to all uses of language because they are the means by which we conceptualize relations between signifiers and signifieds according to a perceived comparability, in the case of metaphor, or according to a perceived contiguity, in the case of metonymy. Put thus abstractly, these terms may seem like paradigm and syntagm. A text is paradigmatically constructed out of substitutions and selections – it works rather like metaphor. And a text is syntagmatically constructed out of combinations and additions – it works rather like metonymy. The sets metaphor and metonymy, and paradigm and syntagm, are not identical, however. They provide language with two pairs of coincidental axes: metaphor forming an axis of comparability and metonymy forming an axis of contiguity; paradigm forming an axis of substitution and syntagm forming an axis of combination.[2]

The language of any text, verbal or non-verbal, can be analyzed according to relations of similarity (paradigm and metaphor) and placement (syntagm and metonymy). What we have been explaining therefore bears directly upon the particular concern of this book, which is narrative. Using the principles of metaphoric comparability and metonymic contiguity, Christian Metz has identified four basic types of textual linkings in cinematic narrative (Metz 1982: 189–90). Each type consists of signifiers which are not restricted to words in dialogue, since film uses visual as well as verbal signs. We can explain Metz's four types of signifying configurations very easily with our own examples, all drawn from a single film *The Letter* (1940; dir. William Wyler). These are:

1 *A metaphor presented syntagmatically:* when two textual elements are equated through resemblance and both are present in a segment as signifiers and signifieds. This relation establishes the textual contiguity of the signifiers, which is why it is a syntagmatic structure, in order to establish the comparability of their signifieds, which is why it is a metaphor. *The Letter*, taking place in Singapore when still a British colony, opens with a shot of the full moon against a dark sky and banked by clouds below. Several moments later, after Leslie Crosbie (Bette Davis) has murdered her lover with her husband's gun, she turns from the body to look up at the moonlit sky. In this segment one signifier (the dark sky lit by the moon) is joined to another (Leslie's gaze) to arrange a metaphor of illicit and secret sexual passion that has erupted into violence. Since both terms of this metaphoric equation appear in the segment, they bear a syntagmatic relation to each other.

2 *A metaphor presented paradigmatically:* when only one textual element in the equation is present in a segment, replacing the other signifier while simultaneously invoking its signified. This relation is metaphoric because, as in the first type, the two signifieds are comparable; it is paradigmatic, however, because the signifiers of both terms are not contiguous but comparable, which is why a substitution occurs in the text. In *The Letter* moonlit palm trees are shown repeatedly to foreground the Asian setting of the film *and* to signify Leslie's passion in a paradigmatic metaphor whenever she is not included in the segment.

3 *A metonymy presented syntagmatically:* when two textual elements are connected to each other because of position or association, and both appear in a segment. This relation combines two terms according to the textual contiguity of both their signifieds, which is why it is a metonymy, and of both their signifiers, which is why it is syntagmatic. In *The Letter* Leslie repeatedly crochets or wears lace (see figures 1 and 2), so whenever she appears with lace in the film she becomes con-

*Figure 1*

nected to whatever lace signifies: patience, coverings, intensity, civilization, femininity, gentility – in short, the cultural value of restrained passion.

   4 *A metonymy presented paradigmatically:* when one element substitutes for another through association or position while simultaneously invoking it, so only one term appears in a segment. This relation arranges a contiguity of signifieds, which is why it is a metonymy, and a comparability of signifiers, which

*Figure 2*

is why it is paradigmatic. At the end of *The Letter*, a lace shawl, shown draped over a chair where Leslie dropped it moments before, substitutes for her, so the two are comparable. But the signifieds of each are combined through association – it is Leslie's lace – not resemblance (so it is not a metaphor).

The final shot of *The Letter* joins metaphor and metonymy in a single segment by superimposing the palm trees and the moon over the lace blowing in the wind. This segment illustrates

Metz's purpose in examining these four types of signifying relations: metaphor and metonymy depend upon and can give rise to each other. Although analysis segments a text in order to identify a particular configuration, an entire text consists of multiple, diverse, and changing configurations. This plurality is what provides a text with its movement.

That final segment of *The Letter* also arranges another type of signifying relation which Metz does not consider, but which we have already raised, namely *binary opposition*. Like metaphor and metonymy, a binary opposition can appear syntagmatically, when both terms are present in the sequence, or paradigmatically, when only one term is present but simultaneously invokes its opposite.

For instance, in the final shot of *The Letter* the lace metonymically signifies restraint while the moon and palms metaphorically signify passion. Both terms are present in the segment, so these two signifiers and their signifieds are syntagmatically set in opposition. By contrast, after Leslie leaves for Singapore with her husband and lawyer to report the murder as self-defense, Mrs Hammond, the wife of the man Leslie has killed, appears at the Crosbies' plantation to see her husband's body. Mrs Hammond is not only the grieving widow; she is also oriental, dark, unconventionally dressed (by English standards, that is), faithful to her husband, silent, secretive, vengeful (see the publicity still for the film, figure 3). In this particular segment the wife is an oppositional signifier set in paradigmatic relation to Leslie. The appearance of the oriental woman generates several oppositions that circulate throughout the film: English/oriental, white/dark, wife/mistress, fidelity/disloyalty, respectable/scandalous, honesty/deceit, silence/speech. Leslie does not have to be present for this opposition to be invoked, just as Leslie herself can function as a signifier of these oppositions without the wife being present. When Leslie later retrieves the incriminating letter from Mrs Hammond, the two women do appear together in syntagmatic opposition.

Binary oppositions repeatedly pervade – circulate through – a text because of the differential field of meaning provided by a sign. As Jacques Derrida states, in discourse "the central signified, the original or transcendental signified, is never

*Figure 3*

absolutely present outside a system of differences" (Derrida 1978: 280). Language is thus a field of play – in the sense described earlier–lacking "a center which arrests and grounds the play of substitutions" (289). As one sign means something – is recognizable as a signifier – it refers not to something outside language but to something within language, its opposite, which refers to its opposite, and so on.

Metaphor and metonymy attempt to resolve the terms of differentiation, to close upon a final signified; but oppositions invade metaphoric and metonymic relations, and any effort to resolve opposition necessarily suppresses it by privileging one side over the other. Metaphor and metonymy erase difference by arranging relations on the basis of a likeness, whether through comparability or contiguity. Such likenesses structure a *homology*, a parallelism between two or more sets of oppositions. In *The Letter*, when the metaphor compares Leslie's passion and the moonlit palm trees of Singapore, it establishes a homology:

$$\frac{\text{unrestrained passion} = \text{femininity} = \text{moonlit palm trees} = \text{Orient}}{\text{restrained passion} = \text{non-femininity} = \text{(masculinity)} = \text{non-Orient} = \text{(England)}}$$

As the parentheses indicate, the metaphor suppresses the terms of difference – the implied superiority of masculinity over femininity and of England over the Orient – that allow each of the comparable terms to mean something, indeed, to be compared. Likewise, the metonymy suppresses the terms of difference in another homology:

$$\frac{\text{lace} = \text{restraint}}{\text{non-lace} = \text{(the gun} = \text{masculinity)} = \text{non-restraint (passion} = \text{femininity)}}$$

The metaphor of the moonlit palm trees and the metonymy of lace instigate a relay of signifiers, with passion, femininity, and the Orient equated on one hand, and restraint, masculinity, and England equated on the other.

This set of oppositions, in turn, allows British colonialism and patriarchy to signify order, while their opposite, the Orient and the feminine, signify the absence of order. The final shot of the film, as we said, places such oppositions together in a syntagmatic relation but it does not resolve them. This shot indicates the contradiction in the various signifiers of femininity. Lace is a metonymy of civilized (English) restraint, and moonlit palm trees are a metaphor of violent (oriental) passion. The binary opposition of Leslie and Mrs Hammond, the English and oriental women, would seem to reinforce these two homologies, but in fact it does not, since Leslie, at various times, occupies each side of the homologies, and since there are as many points of similarity between the two women as there are differences. An analysis of the film's textuality which follows the homologous oppositions of femininity/masculinity, oriental/ English, passion/restraint, etc., would expose how they disrupt the metaphoric and/or metonymic composition of any given textual segment. Such an analysis, we suspect, would discover the instability in this text of the recurring signifiers of gender and race.

We have not been able to analyze *The Letter* in that kind of detail, but have concentrated instead on several repeated signifying configurations for our examples, because it is difficult to present or "quote" a section of the film frame by frame. We can, however, quote a passage of prose and analyze its textuality, using the method of segmentation proposed by Metz but extending the number of basic categories to include binary opposition. Before we do so, however, we need first to illustrate – in a systematic fashion and from a variety of texts – how these principles of segmentation do apply to narrative prose.

1  *Syntagmatic metaphor*

(a) Her face was now one dazzle of released, golden light. (D.H. Lawrence, *Women in Love*, 1976b: 305)

(b) When she looked around she saw the wild and battered and bloody apparition which she recognized as Gowan. (William Faulkner, *Sanctuary*, 1931: 81)

(c) Brett was radiant. She was happy. The sun was out and the day was bright. (Ernest Hemingway, *The Sun Also Rises*, 1926: 207)

A metaphor consists of a tenor, the subject to which the metaphoric term applies, and a vehicle, the metaphoric term itself. In the poem we analyzed above, "faces" is the tenor and "petals" the vehicle; likewise, in the film, "passion" is the tenor and "moonlit palm trees" the vehicle. Each of the three verbal examples above arranges a metaphoric equation syntagmatically because both elements – the vehicle and the tenor – appear in the text. Example 1(a) presents the tenor ("Her face") first and then the vehicle ("one dazzle of released, golden light"), whereas example 1(b) reverses this order, presenting the vehicle ("the wild and battered and bloody apparition") first, and then the tenor ("Gowan"). We have included example 1(c) to show how a set of sentences can organize a syntagmatic resemblance. Although example 1(c) consists of sentences that, taken separately, do not appear to be arranging a metaphor, when put together the sentences do syntagmatically organize a comparison, with "Brett" as the tenor and "sun" as the vehicle.

2 *Paradigmatic metaphor*

(a) He took the plunge into another lie. (Henry Green, *Party Going*, 1978: 445)

(b) Within a quarter of an hour we came to Miss Havisham's house, which was of old brick, and dismal, and had a great many iron bars to it. (Charles Dickens, *Great Expectations*, 1965: 84)

(c) "She sucked the blood: she said she'd drain my heart," said Mason. (Charlotte Brontë, *Jane Eyre*, 1971: 187)

These three examples all arrange metaphoric resemblances paradigmatically, because in each case one side of an equation substitutes for the other in the actual syntagmatic organization of the text. In example 2(a) a metaphoric vehicle ("plunging") substitutes for a verb depicting the act of lying (the tenor) to arrange a comparison. Examples 2(b) and 2(c) also arrange a metaphoric resemblance paradigmatically. Example 2(b) draws an equivalence between the house being described and a prison through "iron bars," a signifier with comparable signifieds (both this house and a prison). Similarly, example 2(c) compares the woman being described to a vampire through a signifier which compares two signifieds: the woman's actions ("She sucked the blood") and a vampire's.

3 *Syntagmatic metonymy*

(a) He was caught in the whirl of a scrimmage and, fearful of the flashing eyes and muddy boots, bent down to look through the legs. (James Joyce, *A Portrait of the Artist as a Young Man*, 1976: 10)

(b) Thus Tess walks on; a figure which is part of the landscape; a field-woman pure and simple, in winter guise; a grey serge cap, a red woollen cravat, a stuff skirt covered by a whitey-brown rough wrapper, and buff-leather gloves. Every thread of that old attire has become faded and thin under the stroke of raindrops, the burn of sunbeams, and the stress of winds. (Thomas Hardy, *Tess of the d'Urbervilles*, 1964: 298)

These are examples of metonymic structures with both terms present. Example 3(a) syntagmatically organizes a complex sequence of metonymic relations: "scrimmage" at once signifies *and* is signified by "eyes," "boots," and "legs"; "boots," furthermore, is a synecdoche of "legs"; and "eyes," "boots," "legs," and "whirl" are synecdoches of "scrimmage." This example suggests the degree to which description heavily relies on syntagmatic metonymy, a point made even more evident by the next example. 3(b) describes a setting through a series of metonymic relations, beginning with the one between "a figure" and "the landscape" of which it is "part." The figure is "a field-woman," a compound signifier which repeats the metonymic conjunction of figure and landscape. The "field-woman," in turn, is signified by attire ("winter guise"), which is metonymically broken down even further ("cap," "cravat," "skirt," "wrapper," "gloves"), and then still further ("grey serge," "red woollen," etc.), almost to the point of disintegration ("Every thread," which then metonymically resignifies the whole: "old attire"). Likewise, the landscape is depicted through a series of metonymic signifiers ("raindrops," "sunbeams," "winds") that are, in turn, signified by another set of metonymies ("stroke," "burn," "stress").

## 4 *Paradigmatic metonymy*

(a) Is it to be wondered at if my thoughts were dazed, as my eyes were, when I came out into the natural light from the misty yellow rooms? (Dickens, *Great Expectations*, 1965: 124)

(b) The room expelled its breath, sucked it quickly in and held it again. (Faulkner, *Sanctuary*, 1931: 281)

These two examples present a metonymic relation paradigmatically. In example 4(a) "misty yellow rooms" signifies a house (the same one compared to a prison in 2(b)): the two signifieds are contiguous (which is why the rooms can stand in for the entire house), but the two signifiers are only comparable, since "house" does not actually appear in the sentence. Example 4(b) performs a double metonymic substitution: "the room" paradigmatically signifies the people it contains, and those people are also signified by their "breath."

## 5 *Syntagmatic opposition*

(a) Her father was not a coherent human being, he was a roomful of old echoes. (Lawrence, *Women in Love*, 1976b: 250)

(b) It was a large, handsome, stone building, standing well on rising ground, and backed by a ridge of high woody hills; – and in front, a stream of some natural importance was swelled into greater, but without any artificial appearance. Its banks were formal, not falsely adorned. (Jane Austen, *Pride and Prejudice*, 1966: 167)

In these examples oppositional signifiers and signifieds appear together, and this syntagmatic arrangement organizes a hierarchy of value by privileging one side over the other through negation. This privileging is most clear in example 5(a), which syntagmatically arranges a metaphor to describe the father ("a roomful of old echoes"). In addition to stating what the father was, the sentence states what he was *not*, syntagmatically arranging oppositions between "human" and "room," "being" and "echoes," and "coherent" and "not coherent"; this structure suppresses difference in the very announcing of it. Similarly, in its description of an estate, example 5(b) includes both terms of oppositions, and it too privileges one side over the other through negation: "natural"/"artificial," "formal"/ "adorned," and, somewhat less obviously, "importance"/ "appearance." This last pair indicates the degree to which the sentence's syntagmatic arrangement of oppositions arranges them into a hierarchy (this but not that) by treating them as categories of value, the only basis for distinguishing "appearance" from "importance."

## 6 *Paradigmatic opposition*

(a) Her contempt was so strong, that it became infectious, and I caught it. (Dickens, *Great Expectations*, 1965: 90)

Example 6(a) arranges a syntagmatic metaphor between contempt and infection, and between contempt and strength; out of these similarities, the sentence paradigmatically arranges a homology, with one set of terms present in the text as signifiers, and the other cited as their oppositional signifieds: "contempt"/respect, "strong"/weak, "infectious"/harmless, "caught"/free of. We have included only one example of paradigmatic opposition because, owing to the differential field provided by signifiers, all of the examples quoted previously arrange oppositions paradigmatically too. In example 5(b), for instance, the description of the estate cites oppositions paradigmatically as well as syntagmatically. In addition to those already mentioned, the description further signifies the oppositions of large/small, handsome/ugly, stone/wood, high/low, false/true. Similarly, in example 3(b) the metonymic description of the figure in the landscape raises a series of paradigmatic oppositions: pure/corrupt, simple/complex, winter/summer, rough/smooth, old/new, faded/shiny, thin/thick, field-woman/gentle woman, landscape/city street. And in 2(c) the metaphor of a vampire raises paradigmatic oppositions of human/monster, normal/deviant, sucking/expelling, wounded/whole, etc.

In our explanations of these various examples we have not yet been analyzing textuality but, rather, illustrating the basic types of linguistic relations that comprise textuality. Like the film we previously discussed, a prose text consists of multiple, often conflicting, relations of similarity, contiguity, and difference arranged paradigmatically and syntagmatically. To demonstrate the play of textuality in narrative prose we therefore need to examine a passage more closely and in greater detail than we have yet done.

### CHAPTER I
*In Chancery*

London. Michaelmas Term lately over, and the Lord Chancellor sitting in Lincoln's Inn Hall. Implacable November weather. As much mud in the streets, as if the waters had but newly retired from the face of the earth, and it would not be wonderful to meet a Megalosaurus, forty feet long or so, waddling like an elephantine lizard up Holborn Hill. Smoke

lowering down from chimney-pots, making a soft black drizzle, with flakes of soot in it as big as full-grown snow-flakes –
gone into mourning, one might imagine, for the death of the
sun. Dogs, undistinguishable in mire. Horses, scarcely better;
splashed to their very blinkers. Foot passengers, jostling one
another's umbrellas, in a general infection of ill-temper, and
losing their foot-hold at street corners, where tens of
thousands of other foot passengers have been slipping and
sliding since the day broke (if the day ever broke), adding new
deposits to the crust upon crust of mud, sticking at those
points tenaciously to the pavement, and accumulating at
compound interest. (Charles Dickens, *Bleak House*, 1977: 5)

This opening paragraph presents a description of London.
Set off by a period and treated as a complete sentence in and of
itself, the single word "London" stresses the contiguous relation
on the printed page between this signifier and the rest of the
paragraph. In other words, "London" is set syntagmatically in
a metonymic relation to the entire paragraph – it is the whole of
which the details following are parts.

"London" generates a series of metonymic movements. The
passage begins with what seems like a news report with a
dateline: "London. Michaelmas Term lately over." This information could have been presented more directly, for it is like
using the phrase "October lately over" to indicate the month of
November. Why is "Michaelmas Term" used rather than a
phrase such as "fall was over in London" or "the autumn season
had just ended in London"? "Michaelmas Term" is a phrase
used by academic, religious, and, most importantly – given the
chapter's title "In Chancery" (that is, in the court of law settling
disputes of wills, mortgages, etc.) – legal institutions to mark
time. So "Michaelmas Term lately over" signifies that a season
of legal business or duty has just passed and another term
begun. But the present session is not identified – it remains a
buried signified, which, acting rather like a pronoun in reverse,
paradigmatically functions as a metonymic signifier pointing
back to "London" to define the city through its institutions, and
pointing ahead to that sentence in the paragraph when the time
of year is indicated more precisely (though still without naming
the present session).

The next clause includes two more proper names of London institutions: "Lord Chancellor," the presiding judge of Chancery and the most prestigious justice in England, and "Lincoln's Inn Hall," a courtroom in the block of buildings run by one of the four legal societies which admitted barristers to the bar. These names narrow the metonymic equation of London and its institutions to exclude all but the court system. In addition, with this series of four names the text is charting a movement from space (London) to time (after Michaelmas) to person (Lord Chancellor) to place (Lincoln's Inn Hall). There is a narrowing down, then, in location and in the focus on one person and the institution he represents. There is also an inferred movement from outside to inside and then to outside again (the weather and mud mentioned in the next sentences). Finally, this sentence is not even a sentence but a fragment (as are all the "sentences" in the paragraph). There is no main verb, just a participle. On the level of syntax too, then, there is a lack of completed action, and this inaction serves as another metonymic signifier of "London."

With the appearance of the word "implacable" in the next sentence a new textual element emerges. "Implacable" puts stress on the text. In contrast to the words surrounding it, which create an impression of objective, impersonal description, "implacable" suggests that someone has an opinion about the "November weather." But whose opinion is it? And to what does "implacable" refer? Just the weather? What about "Lord Chancellor sitting," since that phrase immediately precedes "implacable"? "Implacable," moreover, signifies various subjective impressions of the weather and, by metonymic substitution, of the inactive Lord Chancellor too: relentless, merciless, compassionless, rigid, vengeful. More of a floating signifier than any word so far, "implacable" moves a reader's attention backwards in a metonymic sequence – to the Lord Chancellor, to Chancery, to London – as well as ahead to the "November weather."

The contrast between "implacable" and the words surrounding it calls attention to a binary opposition of subjective/objective or personal/impersonal. Indeed, if we look back at the second sentence, we can notice how the nouns inscribe this opposition too: the only inhabitant of London mentioned

("Lord Chancellor") is placed in between impersonal signifiers of time ("Michaelmas Term") and place ("Lincoln's Inn Hall"). With "Lord Chancellor" positioned inside the sentence structure just as he sits inside Lincoln's Inn Hall, another binary opposition (inside/outside) appears when the passage moves back outside in the next sentence. Looking through the entire paragraph we can notice many more paradigmatic binary oppositions: inaction/action (from "sitting"), past/present (from the "Megalosaurus"), lowering/raising (from the chimneys), soft/hard (from the soot), black/white (from the same), death/life (from the "mourning" snow), animate/ inanimate (from the inhabitants of London), infection/health (from the description of the people), ill temper/good humor (from the same), slippery/stable (from the muddy streets), and fragmentation/wholeness (from the sentence structure of the passage). The text also arranges oppositions syntagmatically. For example, although the street is filled with "much mud," the effect being one of a flood, "as if the waters had not newly retired," the syntagmatic conjunction raises the opposition of earth/water. And when we first are told that "the day broke," the time of day is immediately retracted in a parenthesis placed next to that phrase: "(if the day ever broke)." This syntagmatic conjunction establishes the opposition of day/night.

In addition to a movement of metonymic relations through which oppositions circulate, there is a counter-movement of metaphoric relations. Here syntax arranges similarities paradigmatically. Nearly all the verbs are participles: not only "sitting" but also "retired," "waddling," "lowering" and "making." These verbs describe slow, deliberate movements, with "sitting" the most static of all. From the parallel relation of "sitting" to these other participles we can infer a similarity between the nouns attached to those verbs. Based on a principle of substitution, the Lord Chancellor is more slow than the flood waters gradually receding, than a large dinosaur, than the drifting smoke. Likewise, three sentences start with just a single noun and a comma: "Dogs," "Horses," and "Foot passengers." The parallel placement of these nouns in successive sentences equates them as signifiers in another paradigmatic metaphor: animals and foot passengers alike get lost in the mud and smoke so that you can hardly tell one from another.

The metaphoric activity of the text invokes oppositions by collapsing them in similarity, and ends up sliding signifiers up and down the metonymic chain started with "London." First of all, in a metaphor presented syntagmatically, the text equates mud and money. In the last sentence mud is "accumulating at compound interest." Equated only by virtue of the metaphor, these two signifiers, one named (mud) and one only referred to by its growth of value when banked (money), seem like opposites in various ways. One is wet; one is dry. One is dirty and valueless, while the other, though not necessarily clean, is at least increasing all the time in value. At another level one is natural and one is a man-made object for use in human society only. The metaphor slides mud and money together, suggesting that there may be no difference between "new deposits" of compound interest and "new deposits" of accumulated "mire." Money functions as the signified of "mud," but what does money signify in turn? The presence of "compound interest" at the very end of the paragraph returns us to the beginning, to the first stressed word "London." For, while Chancery, or the law courts, is the explicit metonymic signifier of London, the metaphor has suggested another, one only indicated by the chain of signifiers begun with "mud": the City, or banking district, where mud and money compound equally. It might seem, then, that law and justice are somehow intimately connected with wealth, itself connected to mud through the metaphoric chain, and all are signifiers of "London."

Another syntagmatic metaphor instigates an even more complicated series of clustered signifiers. "Smoke lowering down from chimney-pots, making a soft black drizzle, with flakes of soot in it as big as full-grown snow-flakes – gone into mourning, one might imagine, for the death of the sun." Here the text performs several figurative turns in quick succession, expanding the meaningful possibilities of "smoke" with each one. The text (1) equates smoke with rain, "a soft black drizzle"; (2) refers to soot as "flakes"; (3) compares "flakes" to "snow"; and (4) proposes that black soot is snow "gone into mourning." This sentence raises differences between the oppositions animate/inanimate, black/white, soot/snow, but then reconciles difference through the metaphoric transformations, which blacken white, conflate soot and snow, and animate inanimate matter.

Yet to what degree can metaphor totally reconcile the many oppositions stimulated by the text? Even in joining soot and smoke, the text collapses one binary opposition only to raise another. That snowflakes have "gone into mourning, one might imagine, for the death of the sun" implicitly cites the difference between life/death and day/night to keep oppositions circulating through the text so that they exceed the similarities organized by the metaphors. Moreover, just *who* imagines the personified snowflakes? "One" could be referring to an unidentified narrator, some "one" whose imaginative vision is the source of these figurative comparisons, or it could be a generalization, referring to any "one" who witnesses this London setting. Like "implacable," the pronoun "one" and the verb "imagine" stress the opposition subjective/objective. They call attention to the increasingly metaphoric language and the longer, more intricate sentences, both set in contrast to the short fragments consisting of names which open the paragraph. Syntactically, however, the entire paragraph consists of nothing but fragments. Are these fragments signs of the city itself and obvious to any "one" who notices, or are they signs of some "one" imagining the city? And, if the latter, is that someone reshaping this bleak world into a unified imaginative vision, or too overwhelmed by that world to do more than record what is there?

Our segmentation of this passage from *Bleak House* has exposed the play of language producing its textuality. Close observation about the text sent us crisscrossing through the passage where we found relations based on similarity, contiguity, and opposition. In doing so we noticed and engaged in the commutability of language. A traditional interpretation of this passage would seek a theme – a fixed signified such as justice, urban life, progress – around which to organize the signifiers. It would rely, that is, on a single, unifying signified which appears "final," standing outside the text's play of language, but which is, in fact, a selection of one configuration of signifiers from among the various possibilities raised by textual analysis. In contrast to traditional interpretation, textual analysis does not perform such closure but instead examines how a text's signifiers never can be organized into a final signified without suppressing its volatile linguistic activity.

We do not mean to suggest that a passage or section of text simply operates as a self-contained system of difference. Selecting the *Bleak House* passage for analysis necessarily closed it off from the rest of the lengthy text that comprises the entire novel. In our analysis we treat the passage as if it exists in isolation, when in fact it does not.[3] The metaphor of "snow-flakes," for instance, starts a relay of signifiers which traverses the entire text of *Bleak House* but which we did not follow because of the constraints imposed by our isolating a single passage in order to read it closely. "Snow-flakes" becomes implicated in the characterization (Lady Dedlock's "freezing mood" described in chapter 2) and in the events (Lady Dedlock is pursued in the thawing snow much later in the novel). Indeed, this passage introduces a host of signifiers that move through the text in just this fashion, combining with and resisting each other to form a network of signification. Furthermore, in noticing the metaphor of "snow-flakes," we asked, who imagines this metaphor? Although we stopped our analysis at that point, our question could have opened up the passage in another way because it recognizes that this paragraph is the beginning of a narrative. Narrative conventions of story, character, and focalization provide a text with another set of signifiers, and these also contribute to the production and disruption of meanings, as we shall explain in the next two chapters.

Our analysis of the passage was closed in one other important sense too. Although we repeatedly drew upon the cultural connotations of words in recognizing the binary oppositions that established what we called the text's conditions of meaning, we treated these oppositions as if a text created them. It would be more accurate to say that a text "quotes" them. In its language every text harbors traces of culture and history – fragments of other verbal and non-verbal texts. Julia Kristeva, the psychoanalyst and semiotician, first named this mixture of signs, citations, and echoes *intertextuality*. "Any text is constructed," she says, "as a mosaic of quotations; any text is the absorption and transformation of another" (Kristeva 1980: 66).[4]

Intertextuality demonstrates how completely language mediates meaning in the form of culturally determined signifiers which constantly invade all discourse. Referring back to the passage from *Bleak House*, it is also easy enough to illustrate intertextuality through "snow-flakes." "Snow-flakes" is a highly connotative word capable of generating an opposition to soot because it initiates a relay of signification involving whiteness and purity. This meaning is familiar – so familiar that it seems natural – and the naturalness with which such connotations come to mind can hide the fact they are not instinctual and universal but conventional and historical. They are made possible because of cultural documents of all sorts, ranging, for example, from Psalm 51 of the Old Testament, "Purge me with hyssop, and I shall be clean: wash me, and I shall be whiter than snow," to Hamlet's advice to Ophelia, "be thou as chaste as ice, as pure as snow," to the very common saying, "pure as the driven snow," to advertisements for soap products such as Ivory Snow, "99–4/100% pure." "Snow-flakes" cites – or encodes – an intertextual discourse that generates the homologous opposition between white and purity, and black and impurity, and that privileges one set of differential terms over the other. Likewise, the comparison in *Bleak House* of soot flakes to mourners encodes not only personal responses to death, such as sorrow and loss, but also social conventions of grief as well: crêpe veils and black clothes, hearses and corpses, and, of course, funeral processions to graveyards. Because of the historical difference between the cultural practices of mourning in the 1980s and those of the nineteenth century, a contemporary reader, when coming upon the word "mourning," will not find the same intertext that a Victorian reader did. And this difference of response applies to "snow-flakes" too.

Analyzing a text for relations based on similarity, contiguity, and opposition, then, amounts only to the first step of interpretation. One must also analyze the text for its narrativity and its intertextuality. The purpose of the next three chapters will be to examine these points in more detail. In chapters 3 and 4 we shall discuss the conventions of narrative which produce another order of signifiers pertaining to story and narration; and in chapter 5 we shall discuss how various intertextual codes invade the conventions of narrative through its language.

# 3
# The structures of narrative: story

Narratives are always open to textual analysis because they consist of verbal and/or visual signs. In this chapter and the following one, however, we must temporally defer further discussion of textuality in order to show how narrative can also be analyzed as a signifying system in its own right. Together, these two chapters will examine how narrative organizes a field of signification and what kinds of signifying units it places in that field.

The structural principles of similarity, placement, and difference organize "narrativity," that is, a field of signification in which the familiar narrative units of story, character, temporal order, focalization, and so on, all function as signs in the same way that words and images do. A given narrative can be segmented, broken down for purposes of analysis. And, as in our discussion of textuality in chapter 2, our analysis of narrativity here will seek to identify the most "stress-full" points of emphasis, pressure, and strain organized by its structure. To be sure, the narrative system often appears totally to determine a given text's meaning by containing the play of narrativity within a closed structure, thereby centering it through a story or point of view; as we shall explain, however, a narrative structure cannot fully guarantee or exhaust meaning any more than a metaphoric one can.

The distinguishing feature of narrative is its linear organization of events into a story. But a story has to do with more than just the organization of events. A journalist, for instance, follows a story (the events being covered) and also files a story (the account of those events). How and which events get narrated are therefore as important as – indeed, inseparable from – the way in which they occur. Accordingly, our examination of narrative will concentrate, in this chapter, on the organization of events, for which we reserve the term *story*, and, in the next chapter, on the organization of their telling, for which we use the term *narration*.[1]

In breaking down narrative into story and narration, we are following a method of analysis called *narratology*. Narratology studies narrative as a general category of texts which can be classified according to *poetics*, the set of identifiable conventions that make a given text recognizable as a narrated story. Narrative poetics outlines the competence required of readers and tellers of narrative. Like language (*langue*), narrative can be understood as a system underlying individual texts: narrative poetics is to a given narrative what grammar is to a given utterance, so a reader's knowledge of how narrative operates as a system partly determines the sense he or she makes of a text. Such competence is not limited to so-called literary texts or even to fictional ones. It is, moreover, culturally learned, reinforced by narratives of all sorts: novels, short stories, and films, of course, but also newspapers, advertisements, histories, myths, letters, anecdotes, jokes, popular entertainments, and public ceremonies.

Since the purpose of this chapter is to conceptualize narrative as an analyzable semiotic structure, we shall repeatedly draw on a small group of exemplary texts in order to illustrate the most basic structural components which all narratives share. We must point out, though, that this underlying structure of narrativity does not appear in every text in the same way or with the same emphasis.[2]

Story consists of events placed in a sequence to delineate a process of change, the transformation of one event into another. An *event* depicts some sort of physical or mental activity, an occurrence in time (an action performed by or upon a human agent) or a state of existing in time (such as thinking, feeling, being, or having). The events constituting a story do not occur in isolation but belong to a *sequence*. Every sequence contains at least two events, one to establish a narrative situation or proposition, and one to alter (or at least merely to differ from) that initial situation. As Tzvetan Todorov explains:

> An "ideal" narrative begins with a stable situation which is disturbed by some power or force. There results a state of disequilibrium; by the action of a force directed in the opposite direction, the equilibrium is re-established; the second equilibrium is similar to the first, but the two are never identical. (Todorov 1977: 111)

A story recounts this kind of transformation of events in two ways. It syntagmatically places events in a sequence to organize signifying relations of addition and combination, thereby operating like metonymy in a linguistic structure. Moreover, events in a story do not "simply happen" in a syntagmatic chain but are structured paradigmatically as well. A story paradigmatically replaces one event with another to organize signifying relations of selection and substitution, thereby operating like metaphor in a linguistic structure. For purposes of analysis, then, a story can be segmented into events, and events can be distinguished from each other (and so identified as signifiers) according to the way in which the story sets them in a structure of syntagmatic and paradigmatic relations.

## The syntagmatic structure of events

From the vantage point of a completed sequence, events function either as kernels or as satellites. *Kernel* events raise possibilities of succeeding or alternative events – what we can call, taking the term rather literally, "eventuality." They initiate, increase, or conclude an uncertainty, so they advance or outline a sequence of transformations. *Satellite* events, on the other hand, amplify or fill in the outline of a sequence by maintaining, retarding, or prolonging the kernel events they accompany or surround. Since kernels are the points of action that advance a sequence, they cannot be removed, reordered, or replaced

*Figure 4*

without substantially altering that sequence. Satellites, by contrast, can be omitted, reordered, or replaced (by other satellites) without revising the sequence. For this reason, Seymour Chatman calls kernels "the skeleton" of a story and satellites "the flesh" (Chatman 1978: 54).[3] However, while kernels may appear to function as primary events and satellites as secondary ones, satellites are as important as kernels to a story sequence. Furthermore, an event's status as a kernel or satellite depends entirely upon a particular sequence and not on the event itself, which does not possess the ability to advance or amplify a transformation on its own. An event acquires its kernel or satellite function for a given sequence through its placement in the sequence, because the sequence is what sets the events in relation to each other.

An episode of the comic strip *Cathy* (figure 4) illustrates how kernels advance and satellites amplify the transformation of events which a sequence lineates to produce a story. This comic syntagmatically arranges, or "strips," a sequence of nine events:

1  Cathy asks Irving why he never says "I love you."
2  The phone rings.
3  Irving answers it.
4  He talks to Stacey on the phone.
5  [While] Cathy looks on.
6  Irving accepts a date with Stacey.
7  [While] Cathy looks on.
8  Irving shouts "I love you" to Cathy.
9  [While] Cathy mutters, "Uh oh."

Three of these events are kernels and six are satellites. Cathy's question functions as a kernel because it raises possibilities of succeeding story activity: Irving could answer her question by saying he loves her or does not love her, or he could explain his reluctance to declare his love, or he could evade answering her question altogether. Placed at the start of the sequence, this event initiates a narrative situation in that all succeeding events are situated in relation to the uncertainty raised by Cathy's question. Irving's making a date with Stacey functions as the second kernel event. This action realizes one of the outcomes raised by the first kernel, Irving's evasion of Cathy's question. In the process, this event also introduces possibilities of additional action (or eventuality): Irving could tell Cathy about his date with Stacey, or he could lie to her, or he could say nothing about it. Irving's admission of love (but not of the date) functions as the third and final kernel event; it raises possibilities of still further eventuality (Cathy may or may not believe him, he may or may not mean it, he may or may not report his conversation with Stacey), but it also closes the sequence, returning to the opening kernel to "answer" Cathy's question without assuaging her insecurity. The third kernel completes the transformation of the original narrative situation – there is no longer a need for Cathy's question once Irving says he loves her – by replacing it with a new situation (Irving says he loves her, but Cathy still doesn't know for sure). This new situation resembles the first situation (Cathy doesn't know for sure if Irving loves her because he never says so) but is not identical to it. The difference between the outcome anticipated by the first kernel and that realized by the third, a difference marked by the second kernel, is what structures the story's joke.

The other six events in this sequence all function as satellites. These events provide a transition between the first and second kernel events; they maintain the open status of Cathy's question; and they prolong the sequence. As analyzed in the previous paragraph, those two kernels bear a consecutive relation (the second follows the first) but not necessarily a causal one (the first may or may not motivate the second). The many satellites which come between the first and second kernels more firmly ground the causal connection between them. While Irving's date with Stacey disrupts the sequence by introducing a new event, one which has nothing to do with the first, the various satellites link that event back to the opening to show it prompting Irving's declaration. The satellites delay the kernel activity of the sequence, postponing Irving's answer to Cathy's question and thereby amplifying his reluctance to respond; these are the events which cast doubt on his sincerity, doubt confirmed by the final satellite event of the sequence, Cathy muttering "Uh oh." The satellites help generate the signifying function of the kernel events for the story – that is, how Irving's declaration does not produce the effect originally anticipated by the first kernel – so they amplify the outcome which the kernels advance, and also help to produce the comic's joke.

In our discussion of this example we have analyzed the story as a syntagm which structures a sequence out of addition, and which differentiates among events according to the function they perform for the sequence, either advancing or amplifying it. We can also study this example as a syntagm which arranges combinations of events. A story syntagm combines events to stress their sequential relatedness in one of three ways. Events of a sequence are enchained (distributed in sequence), embedded (integrated in sequence), or joined (distributed and integrated).[4]

An event is structurally *enchained* when the story syntagm places it in back-to-back succession with another event: Irving answers the phone and (then) agrees to go out with Stacey. Enchaining signifies time as a simple succession. When one event occurs after another they are distributed along the story syntagm in a linear chronological relation. Every story enchains events to a greater or lesser extent, if only to produce a minimal sequence of temporality.

If, on the other hand, the story syntagm inserts one event into the time of another event, so that the two occur simultaneously, the inserted event is structurally *embedded*: Irving talks to Stacey, (while) Cathy looks on. Embedded events cannot be temporally separated from each other. It is *because* she looked on *while* he spoke to Stacey that Cathy mistrusts Irving's declaration of love in the final panel. Embedding integrates events in sequence to signify time as a simultaneous ordering of relations between comparable events.

Finally, if the story syntagm gives an event a plural function so that it bears a relation to more than one other event, this multiple signifying event is structurally *joined*: Irving talking to Stacey delays his answer to Cathy, results in his accepting Stacey's invitation to go out, and motivates his declaration of love to Cathy. The event of Irving talking on the phone to Stacey serves more than one function for the sequence, so it is joined to those other events. Joining distributes and integrates events in sequence to signify time as a chronological and/or comparable ordering of relations between interdependent events.

Through such combinations, a story orders events temporally (i.e. in relations of sucession or concurrence) and logically (i.e. in relations of comparability or causality). "Most works of fiction of the past," Todorov notes, "are organized according to an order that we may qualify as both temporal and logical; let us add at once that the logical relation we habitually think of is implication, or as we ordinarily say, *causality*" (Torodov 1981: 41). Whereas enchaining arranges events simply as chronology, so that their logical relation is casual not causal, embedding and joining can coordinate the temporal and logical orders of a story so that they appear identical.

A story's temporal and logical orders are not the same, however, so they often need to be considered separately. The novelist E.M. Forster used the term *story* to classify a narrative that orders events temporally, and the term *plot* to classify a narrative that orders events causally as well as temporally. "'The king died and then the queen died' is a story," he explained, whereas "'the king died and then the queen died of grief' is a plot" (Forster 1927: 86). In the first sequence, events are distributed along the temporal chain of the syntagm. In the second sequence, they are temporally distributed and logically integrated: the king's death not only occurs before the queen's, it also provides the condition of that latter event. Plot and story are therefore not interchangeable terms. Plot refers to a type of story structure, one which places events in relations of subordination, not mere coordination. This type of logical order is so familiar a convention of narrative that readers often expect every story to have a plot, but that is not always the case. *Alice's Adventures in Wonderland* is a story without a plot because the various events that comprise Alice's adventures often bear no causal or logical relation to each other at all. An episode of *Monty*

*Python's Flying Circus* conveys the same effect of illogical order whenever a sequence simply stops without concluding. A story therefore does not necessarily have to place (or "plot") events in a logical order of causality, nor does it have to complete the kernel action of the sequence. But to organize a sequence a story must place events in a temporal order. Although *Alice* and a *Monty Python* episode both lack a logical order of causality, they do enchain events in time serially.

Obviously, the story sequences of most narratives tend to be much more complex than the *Cathy* example. A prose or film narrative usually tells a story which has a large and complicated *macrostructure*, a syntagmatic organization of numerous sets of sequences, each with its own relatively independent syntagmatic organization or *microstructure*. For this reason, and depending on whether one is analyzing the macrostructure of a story or a section of that macrostructure, it is not always necessary – indeed, often impossible – to distinguish absolutely between an event and a sequence. As Shlomith Rimmon-Kenan observes,

> Just as any single event may be decomposed into a series of mini-events and intermediary states, so – conversely – a vast number of events may be subsumed under a single event-label (e.g. "The Fall of the Roman Empire"). This is why it may be difficult at times to maintain an absolute distinction between the notion of "event" and that of "succession of events." (Rimmon-Kenan 1983: 15–16)

For instance, the narrative of an "event" such as the dance at Netherfield in Jane Austen's *Pride and Prejudice* (vol. 1, ch. 18) recounts many single events enchained together in a sequence: Elizabeth Bennet enters already disliking Mr Darcy, he asks her to dance, while dancing they converse, after dancing she still dislikes him. In addition to these kernel actions several satellites amplify the sequence: Elizabeth complains about Darcy to her friend Charlotte Lucas, Charlotte notices Darcy's interest in Elizabeth and advises her to be more attentive, and so on. Each of these events can be examined in even greater analytic detail as separate sequences in and of themselves. The opening account of the dance recites one such sequence, "Elizabeth enters."

Til Elizabeth entered the drawing-room at Netherfield and looked in vain for Mr Wickham among the cluster of red coats there assembled, a doubt of his being present had never occurred to her. The certainty of meeting him had not been checked by any of those recollections that might not unreasonably have alarmed her. She had dressed with more than usual care, and prepared in the highest spirits for the conquest of all that remained unsubdued of his heart, trusting that it was not more than might be won in the course of the evening. But in an instant arose the dreadful suspicion of his being purposely omitted for Mr Darcy's pleasure in the Bingley's invitation to the officers; and though this was not exactly the case, the absolute fact of his absence was pronounced by his friend Mr Denny, to whom Lydia eagerly applied, and who told them that Mr Wickham had been obliged to go to town on business the day before, and was not yet returned; adding, with a significant smile,

"I do not imagine his business would have called him away just now, if he had not wished to avoid a certain gentleman here." (Austen, *Pride and Prejudice*, 1966: 62)

For purposes of analysis Elizabeth's entrance can be treated as a single event in a summary of the dance at Netherfield, but it is actually a sequence of kernel events (Elizabeth enters, she looks in vain for Wickham, she blames his absence on Darcy), and satellites (before entering she dresses with utmost care, she expects Wickham to be present, she plans on flirting with him, etc.). This sequence, moreover, only amounts to the opening moment of the dance, itself an entire sequence which can be considered a single event in a summary of the entire story.

If we are to analyze a complex story, then, we often have to look beyond single events and sequences, recognizing the degree to which they are not only inseparable from each other but also part of a larger syntagmatic organization, namely, the story's macrostructure. As shown in figure 5, the difference between "macro" and "micro" units is relative – relative to what one is analyzing in the story, whether it is the dance at Netherfield, say, treated as a single event or examined as a structured sequence of addition and combination in its own right, with Elizabeth's entrance treated as an event. From the

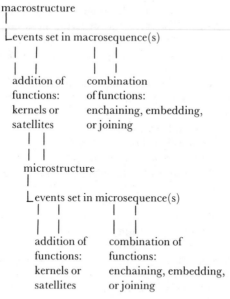

*Figure 5*    The syntagmatic organization of a story

larger or macro perspective of the story, a complex of sequences (such as the dance) can be analyzed as an event according to how it functions as a kernel or satellite of a set of sequences, i.e. a macrosequence, and according to how it is combined in the macrostructure with other complex events.

In a story consisting of multiple sequences, events are enchained, embedded, or joined to form microsequences; microsequences are similarly combined to form macrosequences; and macrosequences are similarly combined to produce the macrostructure. *Pride and Prejudice* provides a useful case study of such a complexly structured story, so it is worth looking at in more detail. The opening event of this story (a conversation between Elizabeth's parents) raises the narrative situation: the five Bennet daughters need to find husbands. Situated in relation to the opening proposition are several story-lines, sets of enchained macrosequences organized around different combinations of characters. These depict Elizabeth Bennet's relations with Mr Darcy, Mr Wickham, and Mr Collins, her sister Jane's relations with Mr Bingley, her friend Charlotte's relations with Mr Collins, her sister Lydia's relations with Mr Wickham. Of these several story-lines the one involving Elizabeth and Darcy receives by far the most sustained attention. It consists of these enchained kernel events (which, as we have explained, can actually be broken down into numerous macro- and microsequences):

1  Elizabeth and Darcy meet.
2  He unknowingly insults her at a dance.
3  She dislikes him as a consequence.
4  He starts to find her attractive, but she finds him more disagreeable.
5  They meet again at his aunt's.
6  He proposes.
7  She refuses and tells him why.
8  He writes a letter defending himself.
9  Swayed by the letter, she begins to revise her impressions of him.
10  They meet yet again at his estate.
11  She realizes she loves him.
12  He proves himself by helping the Bennet family in a time of trouble.
13  He proposes again.
14  She accepts.
15  They marry.

Set in relation to these kernels are numerous satellite events, the dance at Netherfield among them, which amplify different stages of interest and disinterest on the part of each character.

As far as the various story-lines are concerned, the macro-structure primarily enchains events and even whole sequences. Mr Collins proposes first to Elizabeth, she refuses, and then he proposes to her friend Charlotte. There are, however, also exceptions to such consecutive chains; these are points at which events in the story-lines become embedded or joined to the macrostructure. For example, Mrs Bennet sends Jane to Netherfield on horseback in the hope that her daughter will catch cold in the rain and have to stay on, giving Bingley ample enough time to fall in love with her; Jane does get ill and does have to remain there for a time. Embedded to this sequence of enchained events is Elizabeth's visit to Netherfield. She goes to stay with the bedridden Jane at the Bingleys, giving their house guest Darcy ample enough time to fall more in love with her. Here an event from a macrosequence of one story-line (Elizabeth–Darcy) is inserted within that of another (Jane–Bingley), so it is embedded in the macrostructure. When, on the other hand, Bingley suddenly leaves his country house, this event serves a double function because it is joined in the macrostructure (which is to say that it joins sequences of two story-lines). This event suspends Jane and Bingley's relationship for the time being, so it functions as a kernel of their story-line, and it increases Elizabeth's dislike of Darcy, so it functions as a satellite in theirs.

Since the macrostructure of this story enchains most events, those that are embedded or joined stand out as "stress-full" exceptions to the story syntagm's distribution of events in chronological sequences. These differentiated points integrate the story-lines in the macrostructure, setting up relations of comparability, when sequences are embedded, and of interdependence, when sequences are joined. Furthermore, as far as this story is concerned, that the Elizabeth–Darcy story-line is the one to which the others are either embedded or joined gives it preeminence in the macrostructure, establishing a hierarchy among story-lines, with the Elizabeth–Darcy one functioning as a kernel, the others functioning as its satellites.

Syntagmatically, this story organizes a multiplicity of events which it economically places in the service of the Elizabeth–Darcy sequences. That is why the story can be reduced to the fifteen kernel events we listed without any apparent loss. The story achieves its structural economy by arranging the unfolding of events to coincide with the unfolding of an enigma: questions about the status of events in relation to each other go unanswered or are answered only partially or wrongly. Structurally, *Pride and Prejudice* joins its various story-lines through the mystery concerning Darcy and his past relations with Wickham. This enigma pivots around Wickham's attempted elopement with Darcy's sister, and it gets reduplicated in Wickham's actual elopement with Elizabeth's sister, Lydia. So long as the story syntagm delays revelations about this enigma, it can continue to keep the narrative going in a state of eventuality. The enigma thus guarantees the story's movement, while also directing it towards a privileged final signified. As a result, the enigma determines the status of the kernel and satellite events, sequences, story-lines. Further, the points of embedded and joined combinations reinforce the enigma's importance in the syntagm because they maintain its unresolved state, delay its resolution in some way, or contribute to its gradual revelation. Elizabeth interprets Bingley's departure through this enigma, for instance, just as her stay at Netherfield during Jane's illness quietly anticipates it whenever the conversations mention Darcy's sister, the integrity of friendship, and Darcy's "resentful" temper (Austen 1966: 39).

Although a story does not require an enigma, it is a common enough feature to appear indispensable to a story's structure. And to a great extent it *is* indispensable as far as an economy of signifying effects is concerned. Putting ancillary events to such economical use, however, also minimizes the excess or overabundance of eventuality (and signification) which comprises any story and is more apparent in an episodic, unplotted narrative than it is in *Pride and Prejudice*. When analyzing the structure of a story that relies on an enigma, it is therefore important to consider what the enigma suppresses in the interest of structural economy: the kind of surplus activity occurring in the multiple story-lines of *Pride and Prejudice*. They all conclude with marriage, but not for the same reason or with the same outcome; as a result, they each, potentially at least, produce a different signified for the event of marriage, but their integration to the Elizabeth–Darcy story-line through the enigma conceals these differences. In sum, one needs to ask if the closure of the story successfully manages the excess or surplus activity which occurs in the syntagm.

## The paradigmatic structure of events

Our discussion so far has been concerned solely with the way in which a story is organized syntagmatically as a site of narrative movement: the structure adds kernel and satellite events, and also combines them in sequences through enchaining, embedding, or joining to produce a temporal and even logical order. This structure arranges events along the horizontal axis of addition and combination. But a story structure also arranges events along the vertical axis of selection and substitution, thereby organizing them paradigmatically as well as syntagmatically.

A given story, we said to start with, organizes a transformation of events within the syntagmatic space of a sequence. In the *Cathy* strip, the story transforms Cathy's question into Irving's declaration. As the *Cathy* strip makes evident, when a story sequence combines more than two events (and most do), the addition of other events advances or amplifies the sequence to widen the space between opening (i.e. the possibility of an outcome) and ending (i.e. the realization of an outcome). In delineating this space as a temporal movement from one event to another, a story sequence moves towards its *closure*, or point of termination, and yet necessarily postpones it, usually by raising an enigma and delaying its solution. The open-ended structure of TV soap operas makes the importance of syntagmatic postponements quite evident. Serial structures organize several macrosequences, embedding or combining the final point of one sequence with the opening or middle points of another one in order to defer the final moment of closure. Any story requires such postponement of closure because, as D.A. Miller explains, "the production of narrative . . . is possible only within a logic of insufficiency, disequilibrium, and deferral" (D.A. Miller 1981: 265). The paradigmatic structure of a story stresses the importance of closure as a means of containing the movement of narrativity which the syntagmatic structure produces. Thus, while a novel like *Pride and Prejudice* propels its story forward syntagmatically through postponement (organizing a field of commutable and plural meanings for events through misunderstandings, etc.), it also structures events paradigmatically to reach a point of closure where all story movement ceases.

The paradigmatic and syntagmatic axes of events in a story function in narrativity much as metaphor and metonymy do in textuality. The opening and closure of a story are paradigmatic still points of resemblance, whereas the story syntagm moves events in time according to the principle of contiguity. Paradigmatically, what initiates a story is the *placement* of an event in a sequence to mark a beginning; what ends a story is the *replacement* of the initial event by another one to mark an ending. Syntagmatically, however, what keeps the story going as a sequence of eventualities are *displacements* of both the initial and the closing events. Through this fundamental structure of placement–displacement(s)–replacement a story delineates time as a movement (duration) in narrative space (the syntagm) in order to achieve the transformation of one paradigmatic event (the opening as a signifier) into another (the closure as the opening's signified).

The film *The Letter* offers an exemplary case in point. That the story begins with a murder – Leslie Crosbie's shooting of Geoffrey Hammond, her lover – and ends with one – Mrs Hammond's stabbing of Leslie – suggests how the latter event functions, paradigmatically, to replace the former in the syntagm. The events that intervene between these two murders can be read, accordingly, as syntagmatic displacements of the first event to bring about this paradigmatic transformation. The first murder opens the story by virtue of its initial placement alongside the successive events that comprise the story sequence. After the shooting, Leslie claims she murdered Hammond in self-defense; a letter which refutes Leslie's account comes to light; interrogated by her lawyer Howard Joyce, Leslie first denies but then admits that she wrote the letter; using her husband Robert's entire savings, she and her lawyer buy the letter from Hammond's wife in order to conceal it; Leslie is tried for murder and acquitted; her husband plans to buy an estate in another colony with his savings; to account for the missing money, Leslie makes a full confession to her husband; she and her husband try to reconcile; she confesses that she still loves Hammond; she goes outside, alone, where Mrs Hammond and a henchman await her. Succeeding the first murder and preceding the second one, these events displace that ultimate replacement of one event (a murder) by another. These middle events extend and thereby mark out the temporal space in which the story occurs. And the status of the first and last events as the opening and closing of the story sequence is only achieved – and maintained – by this paradigmatic structure, which operates metaphorically in stressing the resemblance of the opening and closing events. The story paradigm encloses the story syntagm, which operates metonymically, for it could, conceivably,

continue, since Mrs Hammond's outcome after the murder
is uncertain. But the paradigmatic resemblance of the two
murders stops the narrative movement occurring in the
syntagm.

Whereas a story syntagmatically arranges events according
to contiguity (i.e. their specific placement in sequence), its
paradigmatic organization does so according to resemblance
(i.e. their similarity to each other). A story can therefore be
analyzed as an organization of selections and substitutions as
well as one of additions and combinations. Paradigmatic group-
ings of events are based on *type*, events of one kind as opposed to
another; or on *location*, events occurring at one setting as
opposed to another; or on *actors*, events involving one set of
characters as opposed to another.

For example, certain events in *Pride and Prejudice* stand out
because their resemblance identifies a paradigmatic relation of
*selection* based on type. When Collins proposes to Elizabeth and
is rejected, and when Darcy later proposes to her and is rejected,
the repetition of an action (proposing) paradigmatically organizes a comparable signifying function of these two events for the
story. (The paradigmatic event, by the way, does not have to
appear in the story syntagm but can be marked by its not taking
place as expected – e.g. Bingley leaves for London without
proposing to Jane.) Likewise, certain events in a story stand out
from others in a paradigmatic relation of *substitution*. Bingley's
departure and Elizabeth's refusal of Darcy's proposal bear a
relation of paradigmatic substitution, since each marks a de-
terioration which threatens the anticipated closure (marriage).
Events that move the story closer towards the anticipated
closure, such as Jane's stay at Netherfield and Elizabeth's visit
to Pemberley, also bear a paradigmatic relation of substitution.
The comparisons organized by such selections and substitutions make marriage the paradigmatic motivation of the story's
closure, which is to say that marriage is always "present,"
placed in a vertical relation to the horizontal axis of the
syntagm, where marriage is always being displaced.

How can a paradigmatic event like marriage dominate the
sequential movement of the syntagm? According to A.J.
Greimas, any narrative sign – in this case, an event – generates
its contradiction, and each generates, in turn, its contrary,

forming a cluster of homologous binary oppositions which provides the paradigmatic structure of any given event in a story syntagm.[5] In *Pride and Prejudice*, "marrying" signifies its contradiction, "remaining unmarried," and these each signify a pair of contraries, "not marrying" and "not remaining unmarried." We can make these terms even more specific. As far as the status of events is concerned in the story, "marrying" is to "remaining single" as "courting" is to "eloping (without getting married)." Marriage is thus always present in the story, if only as the contradiction or contrary of an event actually occurring in the syntagm.

This set of homologous binaries is by no means exhaustive, but it does indicate how the story's macrostructure syntagmatically moves *and* paradigmatically arrests relations between events in order to establish terms of meaning (signifieds) for the story's events (signifiers). The paradigmatic structure of *Pride and Prejudice* exposes what is at stake in this story of courtship and marriage, two radical alternatives which the story's closure works to circumvent: remaining unmarried, the situation which opens the story's syntagmatic movement, and forming a sexual relationship without benefit of marriage, the possibility suggested by Wickham and Lydia's elopement. The closure of the story determines a meaning for the union of Darcy and Elizabeth, but only by suppressing, in the name of narrative excess, some of the other possible meanings (and actions) previously arranged by the syntagm. This closure also validates love – the motive which terminates the story's syntagmatic movement – as the fitting rationale for marriage, so it excludes the other motives – money, which initiates the story syntagm, and desire, which disrupts it – that could have produced the contrary results of spinsterhood or elopement. The meaning of marriage as closing action of the story is thus determined by what it excludes as well as what it includes. Those other meanings can only become apparent when one analyzes the story syntagm to examine the excess of activity which the paradigmatic structure cannot comfortably accommodate or contain in the closure it organizes.

## The function of actors

Analysis of story cannot focus only on the organization of events, since events do not happen on their own. Events require some agency of action: characters, which are also structured as units of meaning along syntagmatic and paradigmatic axes. Story places characters in relation to a sequence of events; and that set of relations identifies the *functions* which the characters perform as actors. The placement of characters in a story can be compared to the syntactic placement of words in a sentence. Each word serves a particular function for the sentence, but only in syntagmatic relation to the other words that comprise the sentence, and only because of the paradigmatic value of the position it occupies in the sentence. Thus in "the dog chases the cat" *dog* functions as the subject of the action *chase*, and *cat* functions as its object. Characters in a story function in relation to events, paradigmatically and syntagmatically, much as nouns function in relation to the predicate of a sentence. Although this analogy suggests that character functions are as determinate as the grammatical functions of words, often this is simply not the case. Analyzing the function of a character depends upon having previously determined the status of events in the story, so differing analyses of a story structure might well assign functions to a character differently.

The *subject* and *object* of an event designate two classes of actors in that they name the positions actual characters occupy with respect to the story. The subject of a story is the performative agency of action, and the object is the goal or destination of that action. Both subject and object function in a *direct* relation to the events of a story. In addition, four other possible classes of actors function in an *indirect* relation to events: the *sender* (initiating or enabling the event), the *receiver* (benefiting from or registering effects of the event), the *opponent* (retarding or impeding the event by opposing the subject or competing with the subject for the object), and the *helper* (advancing or furthering the event by supporting or assisting the subject). These functions are most evident in folk and fairy tales.[6] In "Beauty and the Beast," the Beast is the subject, Beauty is the object, the witch who turns the prince into the Beast is the sender, Beauty's jealous sisters are the opponent, her father is the helper, and the Beast's kingdom is the receiver.

The six character functions can just as easily apply to a macrostructure in a story more complex than a fairy tale. The story paradigm of *The Letter* organizes the following functions:

| | |
|---|---|
| *subject* | Leslie Crosbie |
| *object* | her lover, Geoffrey Hammond |
| *sender* | her husband, Robert Crosbie |
| *receiver* | her society, the British colony in Singapore |
| *opponent* | her rival, Mrs Hammond |
| *helper* | her lawyer, Howard Joyce |

Such a paradigmatic scheme oversimplifies the characters' functions, however, for it must discount the shifts of functions occurring in a story syntagm, which actually organizes differing ensembles of the six possible functions.

Consider, for example, the different organizations of character functions in these two events from *The Letter*:

| *event* | shooting (of Hammond) | purchase (of the letter) |
|---|---|---|
| *subject* | Leslie | Leslie |
| *object* | Hammond | the letter |
| *sender* | desire, the letter | Robert's money |
| *receiver* | the law, Howard Joyce | Mrs Hammond, Ong (her go-between) |
| *opponent* | Mrs Hammond | the law |
| *helper* | Robert's absence, the gun | Howard Joyce |

As these two examples show, a single character does not always function in the same way. In this story the function of Howard Joyce syntagmatically changes from event to event. He is: the receiver of the shooting (since he will defend Leslie); the object of Leslie's false confession following the shooting; the subject and receiver when he questions her about the letter; and a helper when he arranges for the purchase of the letter, goes with Leslie to retrieve it, and suppresses its existence during her trial. Notice, too, that a function does not have to be performed by a human agent. The letter serves as a sender (first by inviting Hammond to Leslie's house in her husband's absence, and later by prompting Joyce's interrogation of Leslie), as an opponent (exposing Leslie to be a liar and adultress), as an object (when it is purchased), as a helper (because of its concealment Leslie is acquitted), and again as a sender (because all of Robert's savings have been used to buy it back, the letter finally forces Leslie to tell her husband the truth about her affair with Hammond). In other events of this story, functions are performed by abstractions. The law is the receiver of the shooting, the subject of Leslie's arrest afterwards, and the subject and sender in her trial ("In a civilized society," Joyce tells Leslie, "a trial is inevitable"). Similarly, desire is a sender in Hammond's murder and an opponent in Leslie's effort to reconcile with her husband ("With all my heart," she exclaims, "I still love the man I killed!"). The protagonist of a story, finally, is not always or necessarily the subject of its action. Leslie's function as an actor alternates between subject and object at various points in the story. In the opening event, when Leslie shoots Hammond, she is the subject of the action and he is the object, while in later events, when Joyce interrogates her about the letter, or when Mrs Hammond stabs her, she is the object to their subjects.

Since a single character is a syntagmatic organization of functions, the characters in a story can be analyzed on the basis of their performing: *singular functions*, when a character serves the same function repeatedly; *changing functions*, when a character serves a different function for different events; *multiple functions*, when a character serves more than one function for an event; or *indeterminate functions*, when the function of a character is not apparent or is revised in retrospect.

Shifts in functions mark out an unstable field of character signification, since each event rearranges the differential relations between characters. An analysis of functions can therefore identify certain "stress-full" points in the story syntagm. In *The Letter* Joyce serves as receiver along with the law in the opening, but, when the letter becomes Leslie's object, she places him, her helper, at odds with the law, her opponent. Her status as a subject of action poses a threat to the law because she divides the law from its representative, the lawyer. The shifting functions of the letter – from sender, to opponent, to object, to helper, to sender – further chart the story's repositioning of Leslie as an actor in relation to Joyce and the law. As the metonymic signifier of her desire and guilt, the letter threatens to expose the fraudulence of the institution ("civilized society") which seeks to preserve the illusion of Leslie's fidelity and innocence. And since the letter empowers Leslie to act – it functions along with desire as the sender in the first murder – the loss and concealment of the letter jeopardize her position as subject of the story. We can thus conclude that the story transforms Leslie's function from subject (in the opening) to object (in the closing) in order to contain the threat to the law she continually raises whenever she acts as the subject of an event. Indeed, we can go even further to consider how and why this story engenders the characters performing these functions, equating the law with masculine actors and desire with feminine ones. Gender is arguably irrelevant to character functions themselves, but it does raise consideration of another fundamental way in which a story places characters in a signifying field: through traiting.

## The traiting of actors

In addition to performing functions for a story, characters are also differentiated according to semantic features which readers interpret as *traits*. Seymour Chatman defines *trait* as "a narrative adjective . . . labeling a personal quality of a character, as it persists over part or whole of the story." Character is, according to Chatman, "a paradigm of traits,"

> a vertical assemblage intersecting the syntagmatic chain of events that comprise the plot. . . . Unlike events, traits are not in the temporal chain, but coexist with the whole or a large portion of it. Events travel as vectors, "horizontally" from earlier to later. Traits, on the other hand, extend over the time spans staked out by the events. They are *parametric* to the event chain.

Thus, while Chatman recognizes that a trait "may either unfold, that is, emerge earlier or later in the course of the story, or . . . may disappear and be replaced by another," he argues that "the whole set of a character's traits established up to that moment is [paradigmatically] available to the audience" (Chatman 1978: 125–9).

In spite of the seeming individuation of character through traits, the range of traits in a given narrative and their effect of differentiating among characters are not based on the psychological individuality or essence of a given character's "human nature"; rather, traits cite a historical culture's assumptions of what qualities are recognizable as "human nature." These qualities are categories of value which change over time. Today's romance heroines, such as Tamara from Janet Dailey's *The Hostage Bride*, have our own culture's preferred female body, one which calls to mind the regimen of aerobic classes and diets. The description emphasizes "the nipped-in slimness of her waist," "the slender curve of her hips," and "the thrusting firmness of her breasts" (Dailey 1981: 27–8). By contrast, in the early nineteenth century, the trait "stout" describing Lydia Bennet (Austen 1966: 31) gathered connotations of firm and amiable, not fat and undesirable, as it does today.

The exclusion as well as inclusion of certain traits in a given text indicates the terms of value by which a culture represents human nature. So too does the attention to individuality over type in the nineteenth- and twentieth-century novel, as opposed to those narratives from other historical cultures – such as medieval allegory and oral folk tales – which represent characters only in terms of pre-defined categories such as social types or moral abstractions. In any narrative, this is to say, the traiting of character draws upon historically different frames of reference which a culture uses to construct notions of identity. If it seems natural today to read and write about character as individual essence, that is because such an assumption about identity is historically bound to our particular culture and its values. In fact, it is more precise to say that traits are not psychological features but semantic features (or *semes*), which refer, not to an essentialized and universal human nature, but "to a stock of physical, behavioural, psychological and verbal attributes out of which fictional characters may be put together" (Fowler 1977: 35).

How do we recognize a trait? Rimmon-Kenan explains that various "textual indicators of character" define traits directly or present them indirectly (Rimmon-Kenan 1983: 59). Traits stated directly may appear briefly in the form of epithets linked to the character's name (adjectives or adverbs) or more fully in descriptions. Sometimes a name itself directly signifies the trait either through a paradigmatic metonymy (Beauty, Allworthy,

Green Knight, etc.) or through a paradigmatic metaphor (Angel Clare, Stephen Dedalus, Michael Knight, etc.). Traits stated indirectly are implied by actions and dialogue, or by analogy to traits attributed to other characters. Lydia Bennet, for example, is "stout," "well-grown," "fifteen," has "a fine complexion and good-humoured countenance," "high animal spirits," "a sort of natural self-consequence," and "easy manners" (Austen 1966: 31). These traits are assigned to Lydia in an instance of direct statement: she "equals" the description which qualifies her name. Here the relation between the name and the trait is established on the basis of explicit contiguity. By contrast, Lydia's elopement with Wickham is an indirect statement of recklessness: Lydia's personality resembles her action (and can thus be understood to be a cause of it). Here the relation between name and trait is established on the basis of an implicit comparison between one type of signifier (an action) and another (the characteristic trait).

The traiting of character paradigmatically establishes the field of difference in which characters appear to be individuated as actors in a story. The repetition of traits confirms the consistency of a character, just as an alteration announces a change or development in the character, and the number and variety indicate simplicity ("flatness") or complexity ("roundness"). Elizabeth Bennet achieves "depth" and "individuality" as a character because, in contrast to other characters, she displays a more extensive and changing array of traits. Her traits range from her "lovely, playful disposition, which delighted in anything ridiculous" (Austen 1966: 7) and her "quickness of observation" (9); to her being "blind, partial, prejudiced, absurd" after reading Darcy's letter (143); to her feeling "humbled" and "grieved" at the thought of losing Darcy's good opinion because of Lydia's actions (213). The traiting of Lydia, on the other hand, remains consistent. Even after her marriage, "Lydia was Lydia still; untamed, unabashed, wild, noisy, and fearless" (216). In contrast to Elizabeth, Lydia appears as less of an "individual" and much more of a "type."

A given trait, furthermore, appears to be relatively fixed as a continuously present feature of a character only so long as the syntagmatic presentation of traits is conceived of paradigmatically. Characterization assembles traits at a proper name so that the name can serve as a substitution for those traits (this is the reasoning behind Chatman's claim that a character is a paradigm of traits). The traits themselves do not belong solely to one proper name but circulate among the various characters of a story. The traits attributed to Lydia Bennet do not belong exclusively to her. Lydia is "a most determined talker" (53), and so too is Lady Catherine: "She was not rendered formidable by silence" (112). When the ladies return to the drawing-room after a typical dinner evening at Rosings, "there was little to be done but to hear Lady Catherine talk" (113). Similarly, Mrs Bennet is traited as talkative and even more like Lydia. In fact, Lydia and Mrs Bennet are almost the same character just named differently. On Lydia's wedding day, their difference as characters collapses: "The bride and her mother could neither of them talk fast enough" (216). Wickham is also as talkative as Lydia. With "a happy readiness of conversation" (50), he "boasted" with "impropriety," "indelicacy," and "inconsistency," "putting himself forward" (142-3), just as Lydia does when she returns home after their marriage.

The traits circulating in a narrative distinguish one character from another relationally. Although Lydia shares with Lady Catherine and Mrs Bennet the trait of talkativeness, she differs from them by the trait of "fifteen." They differ from her in that Mrs Bennet is older and in that Lady Catherine is of a superior rank. On the same principle, Lydia shares the trait of talkativeness with Wickham but differs from him in that she is female while he is male, and in that his readiness of conversation covers up his dishonesty. Furthermore, some characters, such as Jane and Bingley, are marked precisely by the lack of this trait, and others, such as Elizabeth and Darcy, are marked with a qualification: when they talk, they not only have something to say, they listen too. For each character the presence, absence, or modification of the trait talkativeness combines with other traits to establish finer distinctions (e.g. dominating, silly, ignorant, pompous, clever, witty, etc.).

Traits thus provide the paradigmatic ground of comparability and selection in which characters move syntagmatically as actors in the story. The matching of traits to functions (in terms of subject, object, etc., of kernel or satellite events) marks certain events as signifiers over others because of the value it assigns to events.

In *Pride and Prejudice*, the comparable functions and differential traiting of character further exposes how the story transforms one set of motives for marrying into another. Darcy and Elizabeth, Bingley and Jane, Wickham and Lydia, Collins and Charlotte are traited differentially and yet also function as subjects and objects, at various points in the syntagm, of the paradigmatic event, marriage. While at first glance these characters all seem to organize the same simple opposition – marrying for love or for money – the similarity of function and multiplication of traiting specify additional terms of difference: love/no love, respectability/scandal, knowledge/ignorance, wealth/poverty. The terms of each homologous binary acquire positive or negative value in relation to marriage, the paradigmatic event, with love, respectability, knowledge, and wealth being favored. In marrying, Charlotte and Collins achieve wealth and respectability but not love or knowledge; Jane and Bingley achieve wealth, respectability, and love but not knowledge; Lydia and Wickham do not achieve love, knowledge, respectability, or wealth; and Elizabeth and Darcy, finally, achieve all four. Thus, while Darcy and Elizabeth's marriage appears to reconcile opposition, in fact it merely privileges one side of the story's homologies over the other. Closing with this union, the story arrests the signifying oppositions that have motivated its syntagmatic movement. This ending treats economic motives for marrying (wealth and status) as if they were similar to romantic motives (love and knowledge), just as it closes off the other motives that potentially jeopardize marriage: female independence, as parodied by the "formidable" Lady Catherine and moralistic Mary Bennet, and female desire, as exaggerated by the "wild, untamed" Lydia and overbearing, childish Mrs Bennet. Character provides another way, then, of analyzing how the paradigmatic structure of a story attempts to unify the various oppositions that motivate its syntagmatic movement, since functions and traits keep those oppositions mobile in the syntagm.

## Story structures

In closing this chapter, we want to make some brief remarks, which we will develop further in later chapters, about the importance of analyzing a story's structure.

Our discussion has been primarily concerned with explaining how the structure of a story organizes a signifying field for events and actors. In order to conceptualize structure in this fashion, we have necessarily had to treat story very generally. We can, however, distinguish among different narrative structures by classifying types of story according to *genre*. Texts belong to one genre as opposed to another when they share a similar narrative structure which paradigmatically projects, for a reader, a horizon of expectation and intelligibility based on conventions learned from prior knowledge of the genre. A particular narrative genre can be identified by the kind of events it organizes in sequence, the principles of combination it follows, the functions that actors perform, and the traits it draws upon to delineate characters. The epic, allegory, romance, picaresque, comedy, tragedy, satire, parody, *Bildungsroman*, thriller, fantasy, science fiction, and western are all narrative genres. Each names a model of narrative structure which organizes events and actors into a signifying field according to repeated and thus familiar conventions of story and characterization. In actual practice, of course, few narratives follow a generic model exactly, and many even mix genres to effect a hybrid. *Star Wars*, for instance, is a hybrid of science fiction and fantasy which also includes conventions of epic, myth, and, in its famous bar-room scene, the western.

Genre is usually considered the special province of literature, but one must not discount the social importance of genres in structuring meaning, especially when representations of sexual and class differences are concerned. Although standard treatments of genre read it as an aesthetically unifying and self-contained system that promotes thematic coherence, genre extends to popular fiction as well as literature, and to non-fictional stories as well as fictional ones. According to the historian Richard Johnson, "forms, regularities and conventions first identified in literature (or certain kinds of music or visual art) often turn out to have a much wider social currency."

As examples, he mentions popular romance narratives and public marriage rites such as the Royal Wedding, and epic narratives and territorial disputes such as the Falklands/Malvinas conflict. Noting how each pair of fictional and non-fictional stories follows the same generic model, he concludes:

> there is no better instance, perhaps, of the limits of treating forms like romance or epic as merely *literary* constructions. On the contrary, they are among the most powerful and ubiquitous of *social* categories or *subjective* forms, especially in their constructions of conventional feminity [*sic*] and masculinity. . . . If we treat these [generic forms] not as archetypes but as historically-produced constructions, the possibilities for fruitful concrete study on a wide range of materials is immense. (Johnson 1986–7: 59–60)

A story's generic structure must therefore be analyzed as a signifying practice as well as a signifying system, for historical and cultural conditions determine the actual structures which a given text deploys to emphasize certain values over others.

We can illustrate this point by setting the text we have been citing to exemplify story structure – *Pride and Prejudice* – in the context of its genre, the modern romance. This genre also includes *Jane Eyre* and *Rebecca* as well as Hollywood films like *Marnie*, *Flashdance*, and *An Officer and a Gentleman*, Harlequin romances, and even comic strips like *Cathy* and advertisements for products like cosmetics.

Although the romance is not fixed but, in fact, has changed in response to different historical situations, we can nonetheless offer some generalizations about this genre.[7] Its structure paradigmatically stresses marriage and aligns that event to the story's closure in order to define a woman's social choices as personal choices (i.e. love). This transformation keeps her in the domestic sphere of the home, the site of familial relationships. Through the generic traiting of the female character in terms of integrity, emotionality, and insecurity, the domestic sphere establishes a contrast to the public space of money and property dominated by fathers and husbands. The typical traiting of the male character in terms of arrogance, dominance, emotional distance, and social position reinforces this homologous opposition of public (his)/private (hers) and economic power (his)/ emotional knowledge (hers). Furthermore, while at the syntagmatic level of the story the female functions as the subject of love (and, as love is misperceived, denied, and apprehended, she is also the subject of various postponements), at the paradigmatic level the male functions as the subject of marriage, and the female functions as the object: after all, he is the one who proposes, she the one who accepts. The double function and traiting of the female character results in a transfer or exchange of power at the story's closure, when, as Rosalind Coward points out, she harnesses his desire through love by functioning as the exclusive object of his attraction, his wife. Since this exchange domesticates both male and female in "the realm of pure feeling – borne by the woman – where men's true identity could be expressed" (Coward 1985: 178), it defines the significance of masculinity as well as femininity from a culturally inscribed female perspective. In this process of sexual differentiation lies the genre's capacity to conserve gendered meanings but also its potential to use the feminine sphere to subvert them if the closure cannot totally contain the signifying activity raised by the story syntagm.

The advantages of analyzing a story in terms of its genre are several. First of all, a genre identifies the cultural semiotics of a story, thereby making its narrative signs publicly intelligible, not only as a story with a structured framework of meaning (which identifies its narrative signifiers), but also one with a social framework as well (which identifies its narrative signifieds). The modern romance genre can be more properly termed a "feminine narrative." For it structures the meaning of gender difference through a narrative representation of female subjectivity in much the same way that masculine narratives such as the thriller and western structure the meaning of gender difference through narrative representations of male subjectivity. Though their structures differ, both feminine and masculine narrative genres rationalize the normative values of heterosexual relations – in the household (for the female) and in the workplace (for the male). In the case of feminine narrative, the story places gender in a field of signification so that, at the level of events and actors, representations of sexual difference acquire meaning by reinforcing the values of love and marriage, of emotional vulnerability and domesticity, and by making them appear natural, inevitable, and desirable as culturally legible signs of "femininity." In the case of masculine narrative, the story structure promotes the values of competition, physical power, and authority as irrefutable signs of "masculinity."

Second, calling attention to the way in which the story conforms to but also subverts a generic paradigm highlights the contradictions in and disruptions of the very meanings which the genre promotes as a cultural semiotic. In her recent book on the politics of gender in the novel, Nancy Armstrong explains how the union of Elizabeth and Darcy (1) transforms their class differences into gender differences, (2) personalizes gender difference as "qualities of mind," and (3) then relocates Elizabeth at Darcy's ancestral home, thereby maintaining "the continuity of traditional political authority" through its historically specific sign – the gentry's country estate – "while appearing to broaden its social base by granting Elizabeth authority of a strictly female kind" (Armstrong 1987: 51, 53). Moments of exclusion, like the ones we pointed to earlier in this chapter, put in jeopardy the class-bound representations of masculinity and femininity apparently stabilized in the story's closure, where gender difference works to reconcile class difference but in fact conceals class power.

Third, analysis of the specific way in which a story reproduces the paradigmatic structure of a genre makes evident the historical timeliness of its sexual and class meanings. Whereas the union of Elizabeth and Darcy closes the narrative by making sexual differences socially equal, and social differences reconcilable through traditional sources of economic power, the closures of similarly structured narratives written just thirty-five years later are not as ameliorating. In contrast to *Pride and Prejudice*, published in 1813, Charlotte Brontë's *Jane Eyre*, published in 1847, closes with a marriage that excludes much more than it synthesizes. When Jane finally marries Edward Rochester, their union significantly differs from Elizabeth and Darcy's. Rochester has been blinded and maimed, made physically dependent upon Jane, while she has been made financially independent. Even more to our point here, marriage removes them from the traditional ancestral country house, and their new home is depicted as a domestic retreat from society rather than as a center of social activity and power. Armstrong accounts for this difference by citing the social unrest occurring in industrial centres in the 1840s, arguing that it made the crossing of social boundaries more politically dangerous to imagine. In these later narratives, she observes, male and female no longer appear as "complementary halves of the same political structure" but instead "represent competing [social as well as sexual] forces" (Armstrong 1987: 54–5). The comparability of the sexual and social relations in the cultural semiotic of the genre remains operative, but marriage, the paradigmatic event, signifies differently. It no longer resolves the problem of social heterogeneity, nor can it so successfully contain female desire in the name of gender equality.

We can offer another historical contrast to *Pride and Prejudice* by turning to a much more contemporary example, 1980s Harlequin romances. Responding both to the actual economic situation of contemporary women and to feminism, so Leslie Rabine points out, these stories repeatedly feature a female character torn between the claims of love and employment. Not only does the female work in these narratives, but the male figure is frequently her boss as well as her lover. Collapsing the nineteenth-century distinction between the spheres of female domesticity and male power, Harlequins depict femininity in a more obviously threatening and disrupting light. Tamara, in *The Hostage Bride* (Dailey 1981), for example, is professionally competent, ravishingly beautiful – and an embezzler. As a subject of action, she poses an economic as well as sexual danger to her employer, Bick. Sexually attracted to Tamara while deeply suspicious of her, Bick blackmails her into marrying him, replacing the stolen money so that she will not go to jail. With their marriage, the story shifts from the office to the bedroom, where Tamara eventully teaches her husband to reconcile love with desire. When a "reformed" Bick returns to Tamara and their infant daughter, the story's closure reinstates the social and sexual divisions which the entrance of the female into the workplace has earlier put in jeopardy. The closure thus minimizes the surplus activity of the story, namely, those points of action which concern Bick's sexual depersonalization and economic exploitation of Tamara as his employee and wife. As this example makes clear, even though they expand the sphere of story activity to include the workplace, contemporary romance narratives nonetheless use marriage to contain the threat which the 1980s social redefinition of the feminine poses to cultural stereotypes of gender: as soon as the male power figure marries the heroine, he validates her identity and desire as "feminine" and his as "masculine" by returning her to the home, where she can bear his children.

These three analytic concerns all point up the cultural work which the genre of feminine narrative performs in its representation of gender and class. The genre of feminine narrative is neither just a type of formulaic narrative nor a timeless story but one instance of the way in which all narratives organize a story so as to structure possibilities of cultural meaning. The structures of story, in short, acquire a social currency that goes beyond the closed system of narrative poetics.

We shall be addressing this issue in much more detail in chapter 5. What we want to emphasize at present is that a story arranges its signifying field for events and actors through exclusion as well as inclusion, and that it produces more signifying activity than its closure can successfully manage: hence the importance of analyzing a story syntagmatically as well as paradigmatically, in order to observe what excess the closure leaves out. In making this claim, however, we must also acknowledge the limitations of analyzing a narrative only in terms of its story. For such analysis necessarily assumes that a narrative can be reduced to a paraphrase of events, however detailed, even though, in sheer length at least, the actual account of events by a text exceeds such a paraphrase. After all, the narration of *Pride and Prejudice* is longer than the sum total of everything we have had to say about its story in this chapter. The telling of a story thus produces another type of signifying excess – narration – which analysis of the story can all too easily ignore.

# 4
# The structures of narrative: narration

In the previous chapter we equated narrative with its story, the sequencing of events which can be paraphrased and analyzed. In order to analyze the account of Elizabeth's entrance at the Netherfield dance as a structuring of events in sequence, we had to read the signifiers of the passage as if they were firmly bound to signifieds – i.e. paraphrasable action. We therefore sidestepped the fact that the event of Elizabeth's entrance at Netherfield is *narrated*: it is not immediately present as an event but re-presented in language. We followed the same procedure when examining character traits, noting that they were stated directly or indirectly but ignoring that they are conveyed by a narration. For a narration to re-present events or traits they must be represented by something else: a sign system consisting of words, drawings, cinematography, and so on.

This chapter will examine the mediation of story by narration, giving special attention to prose. As with our examination of story in chapter 3, we shall segment narration into its signifying components to show how it can be analyzed. First we shall discuss *temporality*, the narration's arrangement and display of events in time, which most clearly illustrates the relation between a story and its telling. Then we shall go on to discuss: *agency*, the medium by which events are narrated; *focalization*, the perspective from which they are narrated; and *discourse*, the site in which they are narrated. Throughout these last three sections we shall also reexamine the significance of character; but, instead of viewing it as a set of traits and functions arranged by story, we shall now be able to consider character in a much more complex light, namely, as the signifier of subjectivity in narration.

## Temporality

The events of a story _count_ as significant points in time – as enchained, embedded, or joined kernels and satellites – only insofar as they are _recounted_ by a narrative. Viewing the telling of a story as a retelling treats events as if they have already occurred in sequence prior to their narration. But narration itself also occurs in time (the time of the telling and that of the reading, watching, or hearing too). Narrational time is therefore not necessarily the same as story time. The differential relation between them can be analyzed, as Gérard Genette proposes, in terms of order, frequency, and duration (Genette 1980).

Reading or watching a narrative always requires some degree of comparative attention to the _order_ of story and narrational times, for a narrative rarely recounts a story either in its entirety or in a strict chronological sequence. Even _Pride and Prejudice_, which pretty much organizes a similar or complementary relation between story and narrational times, places some events (the account of why Mr Bennet married Mrs Bennet, or the elopement of Lydia and Wickham) out of chronological order. At such points of temporal disparity in a narration, one has to place narrated events against the "ideal" ground of lineated time as depicted by the story sequence, and this may require a good deal of reordering. A detective story routinely requires such reordering of narrated time into story time on the reader's part by concealing the temporal order of events in that of the narration. This type of narrative, in effect, ends up telling two stories (the crime and the investigation) occurring in two different temporal orders.

Specific points of disparity between the temporal order of the story sequence and that of the narration are called _anachronies_. An anachrony can occupy whole paragraphs or even pages of a text, or it can amount to a phrase which effects some momentary disjunction between story and narrational times. The anachronic placement of an event differentiates it from all the other events that are chronologically ordered.

There are two basic types of anachrony. An _analepsis_, or textual point of retrospection, reaches back to a time anterior to that being narrated, often for purposes of exposition.

1 Danby Odell was in bed with Adelaide the maidservant. She had been his mistress for nearly three years. Before that there had been Linda. (Iris Murdoch, _Bruno's Dream_, 1976: 18)

A _prolepsis_ does just the reverse: it flashes ahead to events yet to occur in the story sequence, often for purposes of foreshadowing.

2 And later on, many times, in distant parts of the world, Marlow showed himself willing to remember Jim, to remember him at length, in detail and audibly. (Joseph Conrad, _Lord Jim_, 1968: 21)

The anachronic status of an event is usually apparent, as in these two examples. Sometimes, however, if the anachrony does not reach very far back or ahead in story time or if there is no apparent change in tense, the temporal disparity may not be as noticeable.

Anachronies often frame entire narrations. The narration opens with a prolepsis by picking up the story at the middle or the end, and it then goes backward through an extended analepsis to fill in the missing time and restore the linear chronology of the story. Some narratives – like William Faulkner's or Virginia Woolf's novels – use anachronies more extensively, folding events back and forth in narrational time to collapse temporal linearity. In such extreme form, the narration foregrounds the difference between these two temporal orders and may even work against a complete reordering of events in sequence so that the story itself can no longer be conceived as a linear structure. When that occurs, the points of temporal indeterminacies which cannot be definitively reordered in story time are called _achronies_.

In addition to order, the _frequency_ of an event also points out differences between story and narrational times. Frequency indicates the number of times a specific event occurs in the story in relation to the number of times it is narrated. In the film *The Letter* the murder of Hammond occurs once in the story but is narrated several times: in the opening sequence and then again in Leslie's various accounts of what happened.

Frequency identifies several basic types of temporal relations between story and narration. The *singular* event occurs once and is narrated once, as in Collins's proposal in *Pride and Prejudice*. Singular events which do not appear as anachronies coordinate the times of story and narration. In contrast to this temporal standard are: the *repeated event, which occurs once and is narrated more than once*, as in the murder of Hammond in *The Letter*; and the *iterative* event, which occurs more than once but is narrated once, as in the summary of Marlow remembering Lord Jim many times in passage 2. Repeated and iterative frequencies can stress a kernel event, but they can just as easily stress an event that seems unimportant to the story sequence.

Repeated and iterative events acquire their significance from the way in which they are narrated. Repeating a single event emphasizes it over other ones, just as grouping events together in a series emphasizes their sameness. A variation of the iterative – which Genette terms the *pseudo-iterative* – gives events narrational stress by conflating singular and iterative frequencies. Events are said to recur many times but they are narrated with the specificity of a single occurrence.

3   And gradually the intimacy with the family concentrated for Paul on three persons – the mother, Edgar, and Miriam. To the mother he went for that sympathy and that appeal which seemed to draw him out. Edgar was his very close friend. And to Miriam he more or less condescended, because she seemed so humble.

But the girl gradually sought him out. If he brought up his sketch-book, it was she who pondered longest over the last picture. Then she would look up at him. Suddenly, her dark eyes alight like water that shakes with a stream of gold in the dark, she would ask:

"Why do I like this so?"

Always something in his breast shrank from these close, intimate, dazzled looks of hers.

"Why *do* you?" he asked.

"I don't know. It seems so true."

"It's because – it's because there is scarcely any shadow in it; it's more shimmery, as if I'd painted the shimmering protoplasm in the leaves and everywhere, and not the stiffness of the shape. That seems dead to me. Only this shimmeriness is the real living. The shape is a dead crust. The shimmer is inside really."

And she, with her little finger in her mouth, would ponder these sayings. (D.H. Lawrence, *Sons and Lovers*, 1976a: 151–2)

Along with the adverbs of time ("gradually" and "always") and plural nouns ("these sayings" and "looks"), the conditional past tense of some verbs in this passage ("*If* he brought up," "Then she *would* look up," "she . . . *would* ponder") indicates the iterative frequency of Paul and Miriam's conversations. The specificity of this representative conversation, however, makes it difficult to believe that their interchange recurs in exactly this same way each time Paul brings his sketchbook to the farm. This pseudo-iterative places an event in a series consisting of other similar events and, at the same time, distinguishes it from them. The resulting conflation of similarity (iteration) and difference (singularity) gives the event a temporal significance that can be realized only in narration, not in story.

In addition to order and frequency, narration mediates story time because of the textual length or brevity with which it recounts events. *Duration* measures the length of narrational time against the temporal span of the story. The duration awarded to events will not necessarily be the same for each of them, and the syntagmatic organization of similar or variable durations produces a narration's temporal pacing. Through duration a narration can stress kernel events of a story, distinguishing them from satellite events when they are given more time in the text, or it can effect an imbalance with story when it stresses satellites over kernels.

The two most common methods of narrating duration are summary and scene. A *summary*, as in passages 1 and 2, condenses time in the narration so that it is less than story time. The textual length of a summary may range from a sentence or phrase, in which case the temporal disparity is obvious, to much longer passages, in which case the disparity is not as apparent.

A *scene*, on the other hand, as in the exchange of dialogue in passage 3, coordinates the duration of story and narrational times so that they appear equivalent. Although some narrations, such as a news report, emphasize summary, and some, such as the *Cathy* comic strip, are scenic, most prose narrations typically alternate between scene and summary. The passage narrating Elizabeth's entrance at the Netherfield dance, quoted in the previous chapter, consists of summary until, with the speech of Mr Denny, it switches to scene.

In giving an account of duration, summary acknowledges the mediation of events by *diegesis* – the telling of events as narrative – whereas scene reaches for *mimesis* – the imitation of events as they occur in story time and as if they did not need to be told at all. This comparison draws upon a longstanding tradition of opposing the showing of events to the telling of them, but it should be taken only relatively, not absolutely. For, as far as narration is concerned, there can be no showing (mimesis) without telling (diegesis); scene and summary merely identify two different types of duration. Acknowledging the degree to which even a cinematic scene relies upon telling as well as showing, film theory has, in fact, collapsed that traditional opposition by using the term "diegesis" in a new way, to indicate "not only the narration itself, but also the fictional space and time dimensions implied by the narrative" (Monaco 1981: 428; see also Metz 1982: 144–5). As an account of duration, scene must therefore be considered part of, and not opposed to, the narration of events.

In conjunction with scene and summary, other means of narrating duration are the slow-down, the pause, and the ellipsis. The first two extend narrational duration, while the last one eliminates it altogether. A *slow-down* occurs at any point when the time of the narration exceeds that of the story; it inverts the relation of story and narrational times set up in a summary by recounting events in slow-motion, as it were. A well-known example of a slow-down is the murder of Mr Verloc in *The Secret Agent*, which lasts about twenty seconds in story time and yet takes two pages to recount. The effect of a slow-down also occurs, though more indirectly, when two simultaneous events are narrated in succession or alternation. A *pause* goes even further to stress narrational time over story time. It occurs at any point in the text when the time of the narration continues and that of the story ceases, for instance in character description, commentary, exposition, and direct addresses to a reader. An *ellipsis*, finally, occurs when the narration omits a point in story time. The unnarrated event can make its absence legible in a number of ways. An ellipsis can be referred to after or before the fact in an anachrony; it can be inferred by a reader on the basis of cause and effect; or it can be entirely omitted and completely unrecoverable by inference.

Perhaps more so than either order or frequency, duration foregrounds the mediation of events by a narrating agency, albeit to varying degrees. Narrational mediation is most obvious when a pause stops the story while continuing narration; or when a slow-down decelerates story time; or when a summary accelerates it. These three forms of duration stress narration over story. An ellipsis, by contrast, does just the reverse, so it calls attention to narrational mediation in a more indirect fashion, by implicitly pointing out that the narration fails to include something that occurs in the story. A scene uses direct speech (in prose), drawing (in a comic strip), and photographed action (in film) to make story and narration appear equivalent, but it cannot completely efface all signs of narrational mediation. Dialogue, after all, is quoted in prose, often with adverbs modifying the tags "he said" or "she said," just as it is put in balloons in a comic, and recorded by a camera and then edited on a sound track in a film. So a scene, too, registers the implicit mediation of a narrating agency.

## Narrating agency

The temporal order, frequency, and duration of events in a narration always display, even if only indirectly, a *narrating agency*, some medium of transmitting the story through telling. In film, the camera serves as the narrating agency: it *is* the actual medium of transmission. The question of agency is more complicated in prose. By identifying a narrator responsible for the telling, prose narration often calls attention to its status as an utterance originated by a person. Prose therefore encourages what we shall argue is a false distinction between agency (the linguistic medium of the narration) and agent (someone – a narrator – recounting the story through that medium). When we use the term *narrating agent* or *narrator*, we mean to implicate agent in agency, defining them jointly as: the position of telling inscribed in language use, that is, in discourse.

Traditional criticism tries to keep agent and agency separate, classifying narrators through linguistic designation: first- or third-person pronouns. When a narrator is also a character in the story, however peripheral, the narration is *character-bound*, told in the *first person* (so named because a first-person pronoun – *I* – is used to refer to the character who also narrates), as in these examples:

4 What a consternation of soul was mine that dreary afternoon! How all my brain was in tumult, and all my heart in insurrection! Yet in what darkness, what dense ignorance, was the mental battle fought! I could not answer the ceaseless inward question – *why* I thus suffered; now, at the distance of – I will not say how many years, I see it clearly. (Charlotte Brontë, *Jane Eyre*, 1971: 12)

Buenos Aires, June 30, 1947

5 Dear Mrs Etchepare:

I've just had the joy of getting your letter ahead of time, but what a disappointment when I read it and realized that you hadn't gotten the last one I sent. I wrote it over a week ago, what could have happened? I'm afraid someone might have taken it out of the box, how do you manage it so that Celina never goes for the mail? or is it that she doesn't know you have a mailbox? If Celina finds out I'm after Juan Carlos's letters she might burn them.

Look, Mrs Etchepare, if it's too much trouble to figure out which letters were for me, you can send me all of them, then I'll send back the ones that don't belong to me. He meant so much to me, Mrs Etchepare, please forgive the wrong I may have done, it was all for love.

Please write back soon.

Ever yours,
Nené
(Manuel Puig, *Heartbreak Tango*, 1981: 17)

When, on the other hand, the narrator is *not* a character in the story, the narration is _anonymous_, told in the _third person_ (so named because only third-person pronouns – *he*, *she*, *they* – are used to refer to characters). The passage from *Bleak House* analyzed in chapter 2 and the Netherfield dance passage from *Pride and Prejudice* quoted in chapter 3 are examples of third-person narration; so is this passage from *Heartbreak Tango*:

6 Thursday, April 23, 1937, the sun rose at 5:50 A.M. Light winds blew from north to south, it was partly cloudy, with the temperature at 57 degrees Fahrenheit. Nélida Enriqueta Fernández slept til 7:45 A.M., at which time her mother woke her up. Nélida's hair was divided into locks tied with strips of paper, kept in place by a thin black net which covered her whole skull. (Puig 1981: 45)

Categorizing narrations in this way identifies two fundamentally different relations between a narrating agent and the story on the basis of inclusion in or exclusion from the story.

This simple either/or classification can be extended further to account for the various hybrids which occur in some narrations. As the passages quoted from *Heartbreak Tango* indicate, a single narration can be told both in the first and in the third person (Nélida is the same Nené writing the letter to Mrs Etchepare). Many third-person narrations frame or alternate with first-person ones. Even uncomplicated third-person narrations at times insert a section of secondary narration by a character, as when *Pride and Prejudice* quotes Darcy's letter in full. Likewise, more than one first-person narrator can assume responsibility for the narration, with the multiple accounts appearing in succession (one after another); or in alternation (one alongside another); or in a hierarchy (one totally enclosing another); or even in collaboration (two narrators telling their story jointly). To a large extent, even accounts dominated by a single narrator cannot avoid inserting other characters' accounts in the narration. Jane Eyre is the primary narrator of her story, but other characters serve as secondary narrators whenever they relate information about events to her which she quotes in full.

The classification of first- and third-person narrations usefully designates the internal or external relation of narrating agent to the story, but we must also acknowledge the problem it poses for analysis. Strictly speaking, a "third-person narrator" is a contradiction in terms: a third person cannot narrate. The pronouns *he* and *she* refer to the characters being narrated, not to an agency responsible for the narration. A first-person pronoun appears to refer to a narrator only because of circumstance; the character being narrated happens to be a narrating agent as well.

We can see this problem even more clearly as soon as we include the additional category that follows logically from the grammatical paradigm: a second-person narration.

7 You are seated at a café table, reading the Silas Flannery novel Mr Cavedagna has lent you and waiting for Ludmilla. Your mind is occupied by two simultaneous concerns: the interior one, with your reading, and the other, with Ludmilla, who is late for your appointment. You concentrate on your reading, trying to shift your concern for her to the book, as if hoping to see her come toward you from the pages. But you're no longer able to read, the novel has stalled on the page before your eyes, as if only Ludmilla's arrival could set the chain of events in motion again. (Italo Calvino, *If on a Winter's Night a Traveler*, 1981: 140)

In this passage of second-person narration "you" are the subject of events occurring in the story (sitting, reading, thinking, waiting) and "you" are interacting with the other fictional characters (Cavedagna and Ludmilla). "You" are obviously not the narrating agent responsible for the text: you are a reader not the narrator. But where is that narrator? Your presence in the text as the pronominal subject of action indirectly calls attention to the fact that *you* effaces all signs of the agency responsible for the narration, and yet, at the same time, *you* implies the presence of some agency other than yourself as the origin of the text addressing and narrating "you." This example of second-person narration exposes the limitations of classifying agents according to pronouns, for in narration pronouns refer for their antecedents to the characters performing the action being narrated.

In order to avoid confusing a narrating agent with the subject of that agent's narration, Emile Benveniste instead classifies narration according to its mediation of story. Narration, he explains, falls along "two different planes of utterance" (Benveniste 1971: 206). When a narration calls linguistic attention to its recounting of events as an "utterance assuming a speaker and a hearer, and in the speaker, the intentions of influencing the other in some way" (209), it functions as *discourse*. Passage 5 from *Heartbreak Tango* narrates events as discourse by announcing a narrator's mediation (the character Nené who is writing the letter). When, on the other hand, "events that took place at a certain moment of time are presented without any intervention of the speaker," the narration functions as *history*. "There is then no longer even a narrator. The events are set forth chronologically, as they occurred. No one speaks here; the events seem to narrate themselves" (Benveniste 1971: 206–8). Passage 6 from *Heartbreak Tango* narrates events as history by effacing all linguistic signs of a narrating agency.[1]

At first glance the terms "discourse" and "history" may appear simply to rename distinctions between first- and third-person narrators. First-person narration approximates discourse by positing a narrating agency responsible for the narration, whereas third-person narration approximates history by positing a narrating agency which is linguistically absent from the text. History and discourse, however, do not distinguish between agencies but between those narrations which display objectivity, impersonality, and non-mediation (events thus narrate themselves regardless of who tells them) and those which display subjectivity, personality, and mediation (some agency is narrating those events).

History and discourse, moreover, differentiate not between texts but between the narrational registers of a single text. For a text narrates as both history and discourse, regardless of whether or not the narrator is also a character. Whenever a discursive narrator summarizes events matter-of-factly or recounts them scenically, signs of agency disappear from the text and this portion of the story is narrated as history. Similarly, a pause or slow-down in historical narration inscribes signs of agency, shifting the narration into discourse.

To a large extent, it is difficult for a historical narration to elude discursivity altogether. Even when a text narrates events as history, their order, frequency, and duration do not just happen in time on their own accord, but, as we have seen, do so because they are being narrated. As Benveniste points out, "the nature of language is to permit these instantaneous transfers" from one enunciative register to the other (Benveniste 1971: 209). Such shifting can even occur within a single passage of narration.

8  The following groups on the left, for the rest of the album, belong to different moments of the twenties and thirties, with the *frequent presence* of an athletic young man *invariably smiling* and with long light brown hair covering his ears. The remaining pages on the right are filled *as already noted* by a single large photograph. (Puig, *Heartbreak Tango*, 1981: 33; our italics)

Passage 8 narrates as history in that the objects appear to determine their description. The phrases we have italicized, however, all imply some degree of mediation of those objects by a narrating agency that is responsible for generalizations ("frequent presence") and impressions ("invariably smiling"), and that calls attention, in the last emphasized phrase ("as already noted"), to the fact that it *has* been mediating the passage all along.

Since narration mediates story in the very act of representing events in language, signs of discourse make themselves visible even in passages of history. We can further argue that the absolute difference between these two registers of enunciation becomes suspect whenever a narration gives an account of the thoughts and feelings of characters. At the points in which a character's perspective obscures signs of agency to mediate the story without narrating it, the narration makes it difficult to identify just who is responsible for the subjective content and language of that passage of text: the narrator who is still the agency of its enunciation, or the character who determines its particular focus or point of view.

## Focalization

The narrating agent of a text and its "point of view" are not the same. Agency raises the question of who supplies the narration, while point of view raises the question of whose vision determines what is being narrated. We can illustrate the difference between agency and point of view easily enough with film.

There the camera (and its stand-in in the auditorium, the projector) is the overarching narrating agency – it tells the story. Cinema encourages historical narration through its reliance on scene, so that "a film seems simply to be 'there' as it unfolds before our eyes" (Kuhn 1982: 50). Yet, in order to tell the story, the camera also has to adopt a point of view; it has to be located in space as well as time. It must adapt one, as opposed to another, spatial position in relation to the events unfolding in story and narrational times. Cinema is not exclusively historical, since it can turn into discursive narration through "shots which suggest the optical point-of-view of a character" or a "subjectively-marked flashback," an analepsis initiated by a close-up and then narrated by voice-over (Kuhn 1982: 50). The camera's spatial position determines its point of view, or focalization, which constructs a vertical axis of space that crosses the horizontal axes of story and narrational times delineated at any given point in a text. The narrating agency is thus set in a spatial relation to the story by means of focalization.

_Focalization_ consists of a triadic relation formed by the _narrating agent_ (who narrates), the _focalizer_ (who sees), and the _focalized_ (what is being seen and, thus, narrated – in the case of mental life: emotion, cognition, or perception). These relations between narrator, focalizer, and focalized are all based on contiguity (the degree of promiximity of narrator to focalizer to focalized), which, in turn, establishes relations of similarity (closeness or consonance) or opposition (distance or dissonance) between narrator and focalizer, narrator and focalized, focalizer and focalized, at different points in a narration.

To illustrate focalization, we shall draw on examples of texts which do not use a character as the narrating agent. We have chosen these examples simply for a practical reason: anonymous (third-person) narration makes it easier to distinguish agent from focalizer. Our examples, however, should not suggest that character-bound (first-person) narration simplifies or even evades focalization. That is far from the case, as we shall make clear when, drawing upon our explanation of focalization in the last section of this chapter, we turn to an example which does use a character as the narrating agent.

Whether or not the narrating agent is a character, then, a text focalizes its narration in one of two ways. The narration's focalization is *external* when the narrator also functions as a focalizer, restricting the scope of narration "only to what can be outwardly observed" (Lanser 1981: 38). The focalization is *figural* (also called "internal") when a character serves as a focalizer, restricting the narration to "what a character knows, thinks, and feels" (Lanser 1981: 38). According to Genette, figural focalization can be *fixed* (limited to a single character), *multiple* (ranging omnisciently among a group of characters), or *variable* (shifting from one to another), although, as he cautions, any description of focalization will ultimately bear only "on a definite narrative section, which can be very short" (Genette 1980: 191).

Each of the following passages from W. Somerset Maugham's short story "The Letter" (which served as the basis of the film) is told by the same anonymous narrating agency but through differing focalizers.

9  Outside on the quay the sun beat fiercely. A stream of motors, lorries and buses, private cars and hirelings, sped up and down the crowded thoroughfare, and every chauffeur blew his horn; rickshaws threaded their nimble path amid the throng, and the panting coolies found breath to yell at one another; coolies, carrying heavy bales, sidled along with their quick jog-trot and shouted to the passer-by to make way; itinerant vendors proclaimed their wares. (Maugham, "The Letter," 1951: 184)

10  The face of Mr Joyce remained in shadow. He was by nature a silent man, and now he looked at Robert Crosbie for quite a minute without speaking. Crosbie was a big fellow well over six feet high, with broad shoulders, and muscular. He was a rubber-planter, hard with the constant exercise of walking over the estate and with the tennis which was his relaxation when the day's work was over. He was deeply sunburned. His hairy hands, his feet in clumsy boots, were enormous, and Mr Joyce found himself thinking that a blow of that great fist would easily kill the fragile Tamil. (Maugham, "The Letter," 1951: 185)

11  Her wrists and ankles were very delicate, but she was extremely thin and you could see the bones of her hands

through the white skin, and the veins were large and blue. Her face was colourless, slightly sallow, and her lips were pale. You did not notice the colour of her eyes. She had a great deal of light brown hair and it had a slight natural wave; it was the sort of hair that with a little touching-up would have been very pretty, but you could not imagine that Mrs Crosbie would think of resorting to any such device. (Maugham, "The Letter," 1951: 188)

Passage 9 is an example of external focalization because the anonymous narrator also functions as the focalizer of Singapore, the setting being described. Passage 10, on the other hand, uses figural focalization. Joyce, not the narrator, is the focalizer of Robert (the focalized). Passage 11 raises an interesting problem of focalization. According to the passage, "you" the reader, not the anonymous narrator, are the one who sees Leslie, and, while you are external to the story, you are being awarded the status of a figural focalizer. You are thus made responsible for what the text depicts, but not what it says; and this radical separation of narrator and focalizer prevents one from centering and unifying the passage solely in terms of the narrator.

This third passage from "The Letter" makes explicit what focalization achieves for narration, the textual inscription of a position for the reader in relation to the story, a position which exceeds a narrator's "point of view" since it is produced by language. We shall take up this point at greater length later in this chapter and also in chapters 5 and 6. For now, suffice to say that each of these passages provides the reader with a position towards the story that is not value-free but, on the contrary, is bound by a particular set of values (as textual analysis could easily demonstrate): white, masculine, upper-class British colonial.

Like accounts of action, setting, or character traits, the narration of dialogue is also focalized and can be diagrammatically presented, as in figure 6. We can illustrate the focalization of speech with several examples from Virginia Woolf's *To the Lighthouse*. *Quoted dialogue* recites a character's speech directly (i.e. as history), without alteration.

"Yes, of course, if it's fine tomorrow," said Mrs Ramsay.

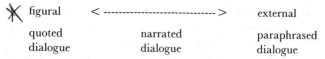

Figure 6    The focalization of speech in narration

> "But you'll have to be up with the lark," she added. (Woolf 1927: 9)

In this case there is no doubt that the character is the origin of the utterance, and the focalization is figural, the narrating agency functioning solely as the medium of quotation. *Narrated dialogue*, by contrast, recites a character's speech indirectly. Enough of the character's own words remain to suggest that he or she originates the utterance, but the narration does not quote it.

> No, she said, she did not want a pear. (Woolf 1927: 163)

> Very humbly, at length, he said that he would step over and ask the Coastguards if she liked. (Woolf 1927: 51)

Since narrated dialogue has the potential to conflate the character's language with that of the narrator's, it results in figural focalization when the speech can be translated back into a direct quotation without difficulty, as in the two examples just cited. When, on the other hand, the source of the language cannot be determined, the focalization is external, as in the following instance.

> And Andrew shouted that the sea was coming in. (Woolf 1927: 115)

Narrated dialogue can thus easily turn into *paraphrased dialogue*, which summarizes the content of the character's speech.

> William Bankes was praising the Waverley novels. (Woolf 1927: 159)

When speech is narrated in a paraphrase, the character originates the content of what is being narrated but the narrator is responsible for the telling of the character's utterance in the text. In that case, the focalization is clearly external.

Focalization becomes somewhat more complicated when a

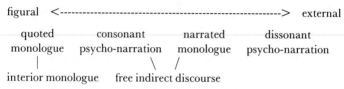

Figure 7    The focalization of subjectivity in narration

narration gives accounts of conscious or unconscious subjectivity: thinking, perceiving, knowing, feeling. Using terms introduced by Dorrit Cohn, we can classify the varying relations between narrator, focalizer, and focalized that occur in the narration of subjectivity according to the scheme in figure 7.

When the narration directly quotes the character's own thoughts or his/her own verbalization of feeling, it is *quoted monologue*. For example:

12 – That is horse piss and rotted straw, he thought. It is good odour to breathe. It will calm my heart. My heart is quite calm. I will go back. (James Joyce, *A Portrait of the Artist as a Young Man*, 1976: 86).

In its recounting of a mental scene, quoted monologue establishes a close relation between the focalizer (the character who is thinking) and the focalized (the character's exact thoughts). Against this relation of intimacy between focalizer and focalized stands the narrating agency, which functions here only as the medium of quotation, the source of the phrase "he thought." When a lengthy quoted monologue appears without a narrative tag setting it apart as a quotation, it is called *interior monologue*. A special instance of interior monologue in first-person narration is *stream of consciousness*, a style of broken syntax and temporal anachrony which simulates the seemingly "unedited" and "unnarrated" random flux of free associations and subliminal thought content.

If the narration includes an indirect quotation of the character's own thoughts or verbalization of feeling, then it is *narrated monologue*,

13 It was unfair and cruel because the doctor had told him not to read without glasses and he had written home to his

mother that morning to send him a new pair. And Father Arnall had said that he need not study til the new glasses came. Then to be called a schemer before the class and to be pandied when he always got the card for the first or second and was the leader of the Yorkists! How could the prefect of studies know that it was a trick? (Joyce, *Portrait*, 1976: 51–2)

Like quoted monologue, narrated monologue recounts a mental scene. An indirect quotation, narrated monologue translates the grammatical subject ("I") and tense (present) of the monologue into an anterior narration (with a third-person pronoun and past-tense verb). Narrated monologue establishes a close relation between narrator and focalizer, against which stands the focalized: the character's self-apprehension.

If the narration goes beyond the character's actual thoughts or verbalization of mental life, then it is called *psycho-narration*. Whereas narrated monologue can be translated back into direct quotation, psycho-narration cannot, so it narrates subjectivity through summary, pause, or slow-down rather than through scene. *Consonant* psycho-narration follows a character's own self-apprehension, often to the point of imitating his or her vocabulary and syntax. From this figural perspective the character functions as the focalizer as well as the focalized in relation to a seemingly effaced narrating agency.

14  The tumult of her mind was now painfully great. She knew not how to support herself, and from actual weakness sat down and cried for half an hour. Her astonishment, as she reflected on what had passed, was increased by every review of it. That she should receive an offer of marriage from Mr Darcy! that he should have been in love with her for so many months! so much in love as to wish to marry her in spite of all the objections which had made him prevent his friend's marrying her sister, and which must appear at least with equal force in his own case, was almost incredible! (Austen, *Pride and Prejudice*, 1966: 134)

*Dissonant* psycho-narration, on the other hand, moves back from a character's perspective to allow for a sharper degree of commentary and analysis. From this position of distance, the narrator also functions as the focalizer in relation to a character who appears only as a focalized:

15 If Elizabeth, when Mr Darcy gave her the letter, did not expect it to contain a renewal of his offers, she had formed no expectation at all of its contents. But such as they were, it may well be supposed how eagerly she went through them, and what a contrariety of emotion they excited. (Austen, *Pride and Prejudice*, 1966: 140)

To distinguish consonant from dissonant psycho-narration, or psycho-narration from monologue, consider whether the figurative language being used to narrate the character's thoughts or feelings (the syntax, diction, etc.) seem to originate in the character herself or in the narrator. In the passage of dissonant psycho-narration from *Pride and Prejudice*, phrasing like "it may well be supposed" and "what a contrariety of emotion" indicates the narrator's detachment from Elizabeth's perspective, whereas in the passage of consonant psycho-narration the more excited, exclamatory phrasing indicates the dominance of her perspective over the narrator's.

Sometimes, when psycho-narration and monologue combine to produce *free indirect discourse*, it is impossible to decide whether the narrator or character is focalizing a particular section of narration.

16 The ache of consciousness ceased and he walked onward swiftly through the dark streets. There were so many flagstones on the footpath of that street and so many streets in that city and so many cities in the world. Yet eternity had no end. He was in mortal sin. Even once was a mortal sin. It could happen in an instant. But how so quickly? By seeing or by thinking of seeing. The eyes see the thing, without having wished to see. Then in an instant it happens. But does that part of the body understand or what? The serpent, the most subtle beast of the field. It must understand when it desires in one instant and then prolongs its own desire instant after instant, sinfully. It feels and understands and desires. What a horrible thing! (Joyce, *Portrait*, 1976: 139)

This passage is not a direct quotation of the character's thoughts, so it is not quoted monologue; yet neither is it a narration of what he is actually thinking, so it cannot be narrated monologue, nor a narration about his feeling of being in sin, so it is not psycho-narration. Rather, this narration conflates monologue and psycho-narration, with the narrator seeming to mimic the voice of the character who functions as focalizer and focalized. For this reason the narration is "free," not limited to what the character thinks exactly, and "indirect," using language which the character himself could conceivably use but narrating rather than quoting it.

Our explanation of the relations between narrator and focalizer should in no way suggest that focalization stabilizes narration by establishing a consistent "point of view" which determines a meaning for the story. To be sure, an apparently "fixed" point of view functions for a given narration much as paradigmatic events do for the story: it arranges a paradigmatic stance towards what is really a syntagmatic structure, not only the story unfolding serially, but also the narration itself unfolding serially. This is why it is very important to remember the example of film, which literally keeps arranging different *points* of view.

A filmed narrative consists of footage photographed from various angles and then edited into a temporally linear series of shots, the textual syntagm composed of differing spatial positions which the camera (the narrating agent) takes in relation to the actors performing a scene. Prose narration similarly consists of multiple, often differing relations between narrator, focalizer, and focalized. These narrational segments are then spliced together in sequence, added and combined in the syntagmatic composition of the text's narration, to produce a continuous discourse, but they also put pressure on that narration by exposing the plural points of view that constitute it.

We can see how rapidly shifts of focalization occur by segmenting the narration of the chapter in *Pride and Prejudice* recounting Darcy's first proposal (vol. 2, ch. 11). It begins with narration focalized through Elizabeth ("she was suddenly roused by the sound of the door bell . . . to her utter amazement she saw Mr Darcy walk into the room") but shifts to narration focalized through the narrator ("After a silence of several minutes he came toward her in an agitated manner"). When Darcy proposes, his speech is at first quoted ("'In vain have I struggled'") but then narrated and focalized through Elizabeth's "astonishment," until he finishes, when the narrator quotes her sharp reply and then focalizes a paragraph through him to describe his state of mind afterwards ("He was struggling for the appearance of composure"). The narration shifts focus yet again, this time to quoted dialogue which lasts for several pages. In contrast to Darcy's proposal, a monologue primarily narrated and textually valued for Elizabeth's reaction more than for its actual content, the inclusion here of dialogue directs attention to a scene of verbal interaction between characters. During their dialogue the narrator seems to disappear, emerging only to include adverbs and adjectives in the tags attached to speeches ("repeated Darcy contemptuously") or to summarize very briefly, providing a transition between speeches ("As she pronounced these words, Mr Darcy changed colour"). After this dialogue, the chapter concludes with a penultimate paragraph of consonant psycho-narration ("The tumult of her mind was now painfully great," quoted in passage 14), with Elizabeth functioning as both focalizer and focalized, followed by a final one-sentence paragraph which makes Elizabeth the focalized, beginning with dissonant psycho-narration ("She continued in very agitating reflections") and shifting back to dissonant narration ("and hurried her away to her room") to close the chapter with a reinstatement of the anonymous narrating agency.

This brief analysis shows how a narration can be examined as a syntagmatic organization of focalizing segments placed in contiguous relation to each other in the text. Each segment arranges a different relation between narrator, focalized, and focalizer. Narration integrates some types of segments to assert their centrality through repetition as a way of inscribing a paradigmatic point of view, but it also distributes other types of segments, which exert syntagmatic stress on that repeated point of view. Given the textual movement which results from such shifts, the narration cannot be centered in a fixed and single point of view or personified by a narrator whose viewpoint is totally responsible for what is said, seen, and shown. Rather, the narration has to be examined in terms of how it syntagmatically sets in place differing relations of agency and focalization.

## Discourse

Intervening with the telling of story, figural focalization also intervenes with the narrator's utterance. The resulting double mediation prevents the narration from being read solely as the utterance of a narrator. For when a focalizer, not a narrator, can determine what is said as well as what is seen without actually becoming the narrator (as in narrated monologue, consonant psycho-narration, and free indirect discourse) the narration exceeds the authority of the agent uttering it but still does not betray its status as discourse. Focalization forces us to reexamine the relation of agency to discourse by effecting a breach between the subject of discourse (the character who is speaking, thinking, or feeling) and the agency of discourse (the narrator who conveys that speech, thought, or emotion).

This separation of a narrating agent from the pronominal representation of agency in discourse, most noticeable when the agent narrates an "other" person (*you* or *he/she*), is the discursive ground of pronouns, *I* included. Like other deictic terms – such as *here* and *there*, *then* and *now*, *this* and *that* – pronouns mean only by referring (literally pointing) to an antecedent located somewhere else in the discourse. To be sure, *I* and *you* appear to point outside of discourse to a speaker and listener for their referents. Nonetheless, these two pronouns "do not refer to 'reality' or to 'objective' positions in space and time but to the utterance, unique each time, that contains them" (Benveniste 1971: 219). Since pronouns mean only because they occupy a position in a given discourse, they cannot mean outside of discourse. *I* and *you* do not refer to an autonomous extra-linguistic individual but mark out the linguistic conditions of *subjectivity*, defined for now as a state of self-apprehended identity through consciousness of thought, feeling, and perception.

Discourse provides a speaker with the capacity "to posit himself as a subject" (Benveniste 1971: 224), that is, to refer to and thus to articulate himself as *I*. Benveniste explains:

> the form of *I* has no linguistic existence except in the act of speaking in which it is uttered. There is thus a combined

double instance in this process: the instance of *I* as referent
and the instance of discourse containing *I* as the referee. The
definition can now be stated precisely as: *I* is "the individual
who utters the present instance of discourse containing the
linguistic instance *I*." . . . [Likewise, *you* is] the "individual
spoken to in the present instance of discourse containing the
linguistic instance *you*." (Benveniste 1971: 218)

As the conversion of language into an enunciation by an actual
speaker, discourse is the differential relation between a *speaking
subject*, who enunciates the utterance, and a *subject of speech*,
discursive elements (the pronouns *I* and *you*) which stand in for
the speaker or listener in the utterance. As Kaja Silverman
observes, "these two subjects can only be apprehended in
relation to each other, they can never be collapsed into one unit"
(Silverman 1983: 46). That they cannot be collapsed is evident
when the subject of speech is clearly another person – *you*, *he/she*
– but it is the same in the case of *I*. The referent of any pronoun,
like that of any sign, is not the same as its signified, which
Silverman calls the *spoken subject*: "the subject produced through
discourse" as the result of identifying with a discursive element
(the pronominal subject of speech) (Silverman 1983: 47). "It is
by identifying himself as a unique person pronouncing *I*,"
Benveniste comments, "that each speaker sets himself up in
turn as the 'subject'" (Benveniste 1971: 220).

   The subjects of speech *I* and *you* lack referential specificity;
they are signifiers of identity only in discourse, actual instances
of language use, where they can apply equally well to the same
person: "the one whom 'I' defines by 'you' thinks of himself
as 'I' and can be inverted into 'I', and 'I' becomes 'you'"
(Benveniste 1971: 199). An individual recognizes herself as a
(spoken) subject distinct from a listener when speaking *I*, just as
she recognizes herself as a (spoken) subject distinct from another
speaker's *I* when addressed as *you*. Each instance of discourse is
"unique," which is to say that in each instance *I* and *you* produce
different signifieds because of their locations in different discourses. In sum, *I* and *you*, empty signifiers which become full
only in discourse, are reversible as well as differential linguistic
categories.

   Discourse, as we already began to note in chapter 1, is not

limited to spoken language, although, as the terminology we are using suggests, speech has customarily been considered the norm of language use, and writing merely a transcription of speech. In contrast to spoken discourse, where the physical _presence_ of a speaker easily allows for the speaking and spoken subjects to appear coincidental, written discourse indicates the physical _absence_ of the speaking subject from her discourse, where a pronoun stands in for her, bespeaking her subjectivity as well as her reader's. For this reason, writing, more than speech, reveals the extent to which language provides the basis of subjectivity in discourse. Constituted – bespoken – with each instance of language use, subjectivity is not cohesive, stable, unified, or autonomous, for it cannot be separated from discourse, the site of its continual (re)articulation in the multiplicity of practices that comprise actual language use.

This theorized model of discourse bears importantly upon analysis of narration. Commentators on film use it to explain how and why a cinematic text operates discursively even when narrating historically to efface all signs of enunciation. The speaking subject of cinematic narration, Silverman explains, "is that agency responsible for the text's enunciation," namely, the means of "production – of camera movement, editing, composition, sound-recording, sound-mix, script, etc." The subject of speech is "that character or group of characters most central to the fiction – that figure or cluster of figures who occupy a position within the narrative equivalent to that occupied by the first-person pronoun in a sentence." And the spoken subject is "constituted through identification" with that subject of speech (Silverman 1983: 46–7). The speaking and spoken subjects of cinematic narration, she continues, clearly "remain on opposite sides of the screen" and so cannot be confused (47). The subject of speech, on the other hand, can be readily equated with the speaking subject whenever a cinematic text attributes to a character "faculties which actually belong to the apparatuses of enunciation, such as coercive vision, or hearing, or control of the story" (48) – whenever, in other words, figural focalization is mistaken for narration. To give a simple example: voice-over narration, a type of quoted or interior monologue in film, appears to identify a character as the speaking subject of the text, since the character literally speaks as its narrator. But,

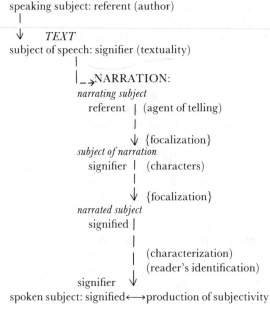

*Figure 8*   The division of subjectivity in narration

since that character cannot in fact be responsible for the camera's enunciation of the text, he or she can only function as a subject of speech for the camera.

In prose narration the differential relation of speaking and spoken subjects to subjects of speech becomes somewhat more complicated because of the additional confusion resulting from pronominal designations of a subject of speech. These, we have explained, function as signifiers of characters, not of narrating agency. However, when a prose narration identifies, through pronouns, a discursive agent (who does not have to be a character), this subject of speech can appear to be fully responsible for the text, especially if the act of telling is also included in the story as an event of speaking or writing. To account for such complexity, we consider in figure 8 how the subject of speech in a narration produces a secondary division of subjectivity.

The *narrating subject* is the agency responsible for the telling as an enunciation. This position marks the precise terms of the narrator as Mieke Bal defines it: "a linguistic subject, a function and not a person, which expresses itself in the language that constitutes the text" (Bal 1985: 119). The narrating subject is not the same as the speaking subject of a text because it does not have the same referential value. Jane Austen is the speaking subject of *Pride and Prejudice*, while the anonymous narrator is the narrating subject of a text which functions as the subject of speech for Austen.

The *subject of narration* represents the narrating subject in the form of traited characters or even simply their functions. At every point in the text, focalization mediates and (re)arranges the relation of the subject(s) of narration to the narrating subject.

Finally, the *narrated subject* is the signified of the narration which results in a plurality of signifying effects: the characterization as produced through the double mediation of narration and focalization, and, as we shall explain further in chapter 6, the reader's identification with the mediated subject of narration in all its discursive heterogeneity and narratological components. It is important to remember that, while some narrations may suggest otherwise, whenever they use first-person pronouns, the narrating and narrated subjects are not coterminous. Rather, they are divided by the subject of narration (characters or their pronominal stand-ins). Further, being the signified and not the referent, the narrated subject is, like all signifieds, commutable to a signifier: of characterization illustrating a given theme, or an implied authorial or cultural viewpoint, or an (auto)biographical fantasy, and so forth.

Anonymous (third-person) narration of the sort we analyzed at the end of the previous section makes these three subjects somewhat evident. In the account of Darcy's proposal, discussed above, an effaced narration (the narrating subject) recounts what Elizabeth and Darcy (the subjects of narration) do, say, and think, and the focalization keeps repositioning the relation of these three subjects in the text. When the points of external focalization place narrating and narrated subjects in alignment, a reader becomes aware of that agency's mediation; conversely, at the points when internal focalization disrupts that alignment, a reader becomes aware of a subject of narration replacing that agency. The rapid shifting of focalization keeps these relations mobile, making it difficult to center the narration or fix its point of view entirely through a narrator or character.

A more complex illustration can be found in a character-bound (first-person) narration, which obscures the difference between narrating subject and subject of narration. Acting as the narrating subject of the text, its teller, the character who narrates also functions as a subject of narration because he or she is an actor in the story. That this narrating character does mark out two different subject positions initially becomes evident in the temporality of the telling. For the character operates as an actor in one realm of time (story) and as the narrator in another (narration).

In passage 4 from *Jane Eyre*, for example, Jane is the narrator of her own story, while her own insights, feelings, etc., focalize what she narrates in what appears to be an act of continuous self-expression. Telling her story ten years after she has married Edward Rochester, the narrating Jane is obviously not the same as the younger Jane, the subject of that older Jane's narration and the actor in the story. Yet it is the younger Jane who focalizes what is being recounted: "What a consternation of soul was mine that dreary afternoon!"

The narrating Jane centers the narration with her "I," and our pun is intentional since the younger Jane focalizes the narration by way of what she sees as an actor in her story; both determine what is said and shown about the young Jane's subjectivity (the focalized). The apparently unified subjectivity of Jane as narrator and character is achieved only because the narration and focalization repeatedly coincide at the name "Jane Eyre," which is just as repeatedly signified in the text by the pronoun *I*. The pronoun *I* thus marks the narration's division of Jane's subjectivity into: (1) an "autobiographical" narrator; (2) the subject of this narration who not only acts in the story but also focalizes its telling; and (3) the narrated subject appearing to unite these two Janes in a coherent, developing characterization.

We can examine this division more closely by analyzing one section of the novel: Brocklehurst's interview with Jane in chapter 4. Outside the room where Brocklehurst and Mrs Reed await her, the child Jane stands "intimidated and trembling," while the adult Jane mediates, remembering "what a miserable little poltroon had fear, engendered of unjust punishment, made of me in those days!" A change in tense, from "I feared to return to the nursery" to "I *must* enter," signals a quoted monologue in the next paragraph: " 'Who could want me?' I asked inwardly." That Jane's monologue is quoted rather than narrated establishes a momentary conjunction of the narrating subject and subject of narration through figural focalization: "The handle turned, the door unclosed, and passing through and curtseying low I looked up at – a black pillar! such, at least, appeared to me, at first sight, the straight, narrow, sable-clad shape standing erect on the rug: the grim face at the top was like a carved mask, placed above the shaft by way of capital" (Brontë 1971: 26). The participles in this sentence – "passing," "curtseying" – especially reinforce the impression that Jane's consciousness as a child is seemingly immediate and unmediated by the adult Jane. Jane's narration, however, *alters* this impression in the next paragraph with a return to the simple past tense of historical narration: "Mrs Reed occupied her usual seat by the fireside" (26).

A second description of Brocklehurst proposes a striking contrast to the initial one of his "grim face" appearing like a "carved mask." Jane is examined by "two inquisitive-looking grey eyes which twinkled under a pair of bushy brows." This kind face, in turn, changes again just a few lines later. As Brocklehurst addresses her, "he seemed to me a tall gentleman; but then I was very little: his features were large, and they and all the lines of his frame were equally harsh and prim." As Jane quite literally changes her position – "I stepped across the rug; he placed me square and straight before him" – she becomes subject to his "scrutiny" and interrogation. "What a face he had, now that it was almost on a level with mine! what a great nose! and what a mouth! and what large prominent teeth!" (26–7)

Throughout this encounter with Brocklehurst, the child Jane focalizes the narration but is a conspicuously silent subject of narration. The narrating adult articulates her subjectivity for her through the pronoun *I*, but so do the adults when they address her as *you*. "Well, Jane, and are you a good child?"

Brocklehurst asks, and she finds it "impossible to reply to this in the affirmative: my little world held a contrary opinion: I was silent" (27). When Mrs Reed warns Brocklehurst "above all, to guard against her worst fault, a tendency to deceit," Jane does identify with that "contrary opinion": "Now, uttered before a stranger, the accusation cut me to the heart . . . I saw myself transformed under Mr Brocklehurst's eye into an artful noxious child, and what could I do to remedy the injury?" (28).

After Brocklehurst leaves, Jane finally speaks out to her aunt. Speech gives the child "the strangest sense of freedom, of triumph," of "unhoped-for liberty," because it articulates her "passion of resentment," making her feel "thrilled with ungovernable excitement" (30–1). The dialogue in this section of narration is interrupted by summary when Jane describes her "frightened" aunt "rocking herself to and fro, and even twisting her face as if she would cry." This would seem more aptly to depict Jane than her aunt, since, from the dialogue, Mrs Reed is the one who appears calm and solicitous, and Jane agitated and vindictive. "Jane, you are under a mistake: what is the matter with you?" Mrs Reed asks. "Why do you tremble so violently? Would you like to drink some water?" (31). Once Jane is again alone – "winner of the field" and, significantly, standing "on the rug, where Mr Brocklehurst had stood" – she loses the thrilling excitement she has felt and "this fierce pleasure subsided" (32). Jane can only sustain that liberating feeling as a speaker set in opposition to the addresses of her aunt, her "antagonist" (30), her "opponent" (31). With Mrs Reed's departure from the room, the adult Jane reinserts herself to narrate and focalize the child Jane from a point of view not too unlike her aunt's: "A child cannot quarrel with its elders, as I had done; cannot give its furious feelings uncontrolled play, as I had given mine, without experiencing afterwards the pang of remorse and the chill of reaction" (32).

The shifts we are pointing out in Jane's telling prevent the narration as a whole from cohering around a unified and continuous subjectivity for Jane either as narrator or as character. Each turn of focalization traces a disjunction between the narrating subject (the adult Jane), the subject of narration (the child Jane), and the subject narrated by the adult Jane and by the other characters as well when they address her directly.

These secondary narrating subjects include not only her ene-
mies Brocklehurst and Mrs Reed, but also her suitors Rochester
and St John Rivers, and her friends Helen Burns and Bessie the
nurse. In speaking to Jane, for example, Rochester describes
her; he thus tells her who she is by subject-ing her to his
discourse. Jane, he says at various points in their conversations,
has a "unique" and "peculiar mind" (126); she is "not naturally austere," for she can "laugh very merrily" (122); she has
"rather the look of another world" (107); she is "poor and
obscure, and small and plain" (224); she is his "wild, frantic
bird" (223), his "pale, little elf" (226), his "angel" (228). Such
contradictory inscriptions of Jane as a subject of narration
further pluralize the discursive ground from which to read her
as a self-apprehending subject. So, to recognize Jane both as a
character and as a narrator, one must follow these continually
shifting points of entry into the text's narration of her.

Foregrounding the way in which a narration discursively
constitutes its account of subjectivity through division rather
than unity, we have pointed out the degree to which the telling
of a story exceeds not only the story but the stable personifica-
tion of a teller as well. In offering this account of Jane Eyre's
narration, however, we find ourselves returning to the problems
we raised at the conclusion of chapter 2. Without the security of
being able to center a narrative text through its language, or its
story, or its narration, what – where – are the limits of a text's
volatile signifying movement? Our theoretical argument about
textuality, narrativity, and discourse will ultimately enable us
in the next chapter to place narrative texts in an intertextual
network of cultural discourses and then, in chapter 6, to explain
how narrative produces subjectivity in a reader or viewer.

# 5

# Decoding texts: ideology, subjectivity, discourse

While in chapter 3 we theorized narrative in terms of its syntagmatic and paradigmatic organization of events and actors in a story over time, we proceeded in chapter 4 to show how the telling, or the narration, is just as important as the story itself. We shall now take full account of what we only started to discuss previously, the location of narrative within a cultural and historical field of language practices. A narrative must be studied not only for its textuality or how it is structured by narrative conventions as a story and telling, but also for its connections to intertextual signifying networks.

We shall thus extend our discussion of the passage from *Bleak House* in chapter 2, moving beyond its emphasis on the instability of the signifier to investigate what such commutability amounts to. In that earlier chapter, when we discussed the following sentence, "Smoke lowering down from chimney-pots, making a soft black drizzle, with flakes of soot in it as big as full-grown snow-flakes – gone into mourning, one might imagine, for the death of the sun" (Dickens 1977: 5), we isolated binaries such as life/death, soft/hard, black/white. Yet we did not have space to explain how we found signifieds for signifiers or why we chose these binaries and not others.

Examining the word "snow-flakes," we just began to suggest its wide cultural field of meaning when we showed how a variety of intertexts, such as *Hamlet* and an Ivory Snow advertisement, offered signifieds which positioned "snow-flakes" in the binary of purity/impurity. We indicated how "snow-flakes" provided connotations linked to purity and how purity always, in turn, connotes impurity. But for the sake of simplicity we were forced to limit our discussion and leave the impression of binaries as largely intrinsic, universal or ahistorical properties, which they are not.

Words signify through connotation, the substitution of one signifier for another to produce a signified for the first. We recognize the meaning of "mourning" in the passage above by summoning up connotations such as black, hearse, wake, grief. Yet, even in the *Bleak House* example, it may seem as though connotation would result in an endless play of signification which could lead us even further, to: last will and testament, funeral pyres, wakes, or Jewish mourning candles, and more! With the possibility of so many connotations, how in any given narrative context can we possibly recognize and agree upon some meanings serving us better than others? In reading connotatively, we are also reading through cultural *codes* which limit the appropriateness of some connotations over others by establishing stable relationships between signifier and signified. Far from being the product of private associations and individual experiences, connotations are, in fact, socially learned and familiar, grounded in what we shall eventually define as *ideology*.

## Cultural codes

A *code* is "an agreed transformation, or set of unambiguous rules, whereby messages are converted from one representation to another" (Sebeok 1985: 465). Codes set forth (*codify*) terms by which one sign stands in for (*encodes*) another, the substitution occurring as soon as the relationship of the signs is recognized (*decoded*). Usually this transformation involves an exchange of meaning between sign systems. A stamp on food or drugs signifying acceptability by a government agency, or any seal certifying the safety of an electrical appliance, represents quality and minimum safety standards in the form of a logo, a coded symbol. Other familiar examples of codes are: the Morse code, professional dress codes, rules for parliamentary procedure at meetings, and the color code for traffic lights which we discussed in chapter 1. Written down as public rules of signification that need to be learned (say, from a telegrapher's handbook, worker's manual, *Roberts' Rules of Order*, or driver's manual), these codes are deployed by all sorts of social groups. There are also codes – such as slang, etiquettes, fraternity rites – which differentiate among social groups, identifying who belongs to the group and who does not by confining the passage of meaning to that group.

Codes are so much a part of our cultural knowledge that we may often forget that what we are reading *is* a code. Signification occurs through all sorts of "invisible" codes, some of which define various social divisions, some of which cross them. Codes of nostalgia and physical beauty, for example, determine what the past and the body, respectively, signify to our culture. The invisibility of these codes results from the ease with which they repeatedly promote and transmit meanings. Although they appear to preexist signification, making it seem effortless and natural, these codes, like the other examples we have mentioned, link sets of signs to what Judith Williamson calls a *referent system*: one of the many sign systems in culture to which a code refers for its "basic 'meaning' material" (Williamson 1978: 19). Authorizing the transformation of one sign into another, a referent system allows encoded meanings to become legible.

A text conveys meanings through its encoding of numerous referent systems. This point can be easily illustrated with an advertisement for Woolrich clothing (figure 9). The ostensible message of the ad is: Woolrich makes products of quality that last a long time. The caption reinforces this idea in a narrative, a history of dependability. "In the 1890's folks who lived outdoors depended on Woolrich. In the 1980's they still do." The explanation of products used – "Quallofil* TOUGH TESTED INSULATION / BATTING OF DACRON POLYESTER BY DUPONT" – attests further to durability. A testimonial to the name Woolrich, the text offers no scientific evidence, such as the actual "tough tested" results, to support its claim. Rather, it cites the referent system of the signature label: "Woolrich Est. 1830." That Woolrich, a recognizable line of clothing established over 150 years ago, is not a house brand or a new brand, like Reebok or Estée Lauder, encodes quality upon durability. In our world of paper plates and disposable razors, the signified of long-lastingness becomes itself a signifier of quality.

To send its message of durability and quality, the ad draws on additional referent systems, appropriating from each system a stable relationship already existing between a signifier and a signified. In this way the ad can then speak of its product in terms of the *same* relationship and values. For instance, visual

In the 1890's folks who lived outdoors depended on Woolrich.

In the 1980's they still do.

*Figure 9*

signifiers of recreation transferred to the name Woolrich – sun, snow, robustness, automobile, and ski rack – associate the product with the idea of pleasure. This correlation is not made by the narrative but by the ad's visually connecting those signifiers to another referent system, in this case to one more abstract than labels, that of nature. The ad promises that ownership of Woolrich products brings the positive values encoded in nature: energy, vitality, health. In the inset photograph which the ad actually reproduces in color, the coordinated outfits of blue (sky) and green (foliage) metonymically represent a fresh, invigorating setting; and, instead of snow, a shining sun radiates warmth and light. With Woolrich connected to nature, and a beneficent nature at that, it would then seem natural to buy Woolrich. From such encodings of resemblance, the ad goes on to propose a further connection between the product being sold, Woolrich, and a second product, Status, which money can not buy but which buying Woolrich can provide.

What we are saying about the coding of signs applies to narrative just as much as it does to advertisements. The question of codes in narrative, in fact, has already been posed, though implicitly, throughout the previous chapters. When, for example, we examined the binary oppositions raised by the paradigmatic structure of story in *Pride and Prejudice*, or when we linked traits and functions to events in order to ascertain their symbolic value, we were placing the text in the context of cultural referent systems. To be sure, our discussion of structure in chapters 3 and 4 pretty much confined narrative to the referent system of narratology. But, even so, we did not assume, as traditional literary competence assumes, that structure is present in a text as a formal support which allows the text to cohere as a work. On the contrary, since a narrative is, materially speaking, not a concrete structure like a building or a skeleton, but simply composed of signs (words and/or images), we were showing that structure is an abstraction, a conceptualization of relations between signs. We can now go further to say that the conceptualization of narrative as an abstractable structure is made possible because certain codes traverse a text so that its signs can refer to narratology for its referent system; and that there are other codes in a text which draw upon a variety of cultural referent systems in addition to narratology.

While the referent system of narratology organizes structure, the text itself is actually a structuration of multiple, often competing codes. Roland Barthes explains this difference in his book *S/Z*:

> We are, in fact, concerned not to manifest a structure but to produce a structuration. . . . for if the text is subject to some form, this form is not unitary, architectonic, finite: it is the fragment, the shards, the broken or obliterated network – all the movements and inflections of a vast "dissolve," which permits both overlapping and loss of messages. Hence we use *Code* here not in the sense of a list, a paradigm that must be reconstituted. The code is a perspective of quotations, a mirage of structures; we know only its departures and returns; the units which have resulted from it (those we inventory) are themselves, always, ventures out of the text, the mark, the sign of a virtual digression towards the remainder of a catalogue (*The Kidnapping* refers to every kidnapping ever written); they are so many fragments of something that has been *already* read, seen, done, experienced; the code is the wake of that *already*. (Barthes 1974: 20)

Instead of using the traditional critical metaphor of "formal structure" (i.e. the work) to describe a text, Barthes asks us to think of it as a braided *text*ure or a *net*work of codes. Granted, "braid" and "network" are still metaphoric descriptions, but either one has the advantage over "formal structure" of not making the text resemble an impenetrable monolithic and solid whole. On the contrary, those two metaphors picture textuality as an interweaving of codes – intertextual quotations – which run through it, often concurrently and disharmoniously. Codes produce the "noise" and "volume" of textuality, and they exceed the finitude and coherence of a whole, formal structure. Hence Barthes's claim that if there is "form" to a text it is the "broken or obliterated network."

*S/Z* offers Barthes's own word-by-word decoding of the "movements and inflections" as they occur in one particular text, Honoré de Balzac's novella *Sarrasine*. This analysis concentrates on more than the single text, however; for, through a rather elliptical and crisscrossing series of digressive excursions leading out of his decoding of *Sarrasine*, Barthes theorizes narrative as a production of the cultural codes cited by any text's language.

"Connotation is the starting point of a code" (Barthes 1974: 9), he points out, and "each code is one of the forces that can take over the text (of which the text is the network), one of the voices out of which the text is woven" (21). A text, then, is the "stereographic space" where codes "intersect" (21). This idea can best be illustrated by repeating Barthes's own comparison of codes to notes on a musical staff. Each note has its place in the composition. E flat, for example, sounds off at intervals. So does A, so does D. These form combinations: harmonies and melodies. Although no code is intrinsically more important than another, Barthes does make a distinction among them. "Connotation," he explains, is "determined by two spaces." Like music's melody which moves forward, some codes are irreversible; they move signifiers horizontally in "a sequential space, a series of orders, a space subject to the successivity of sentences, in which meaning proliferates by layering." Other codes are reversible; like harmonies, they move signifiers vertically in "an agglomerative space, [with] certain areas of the text correlating other meanings outside the material text and, with them, forming 'nebulae' of signifieds" (8).

Barthes's method in decoding a text is to segment the entire text arbitrarily and, quite literally, to fracture it into *lexias*, "units of reading" (Barthes 1974: 13). Each lexia displays certain codes passing through the text, so that at any and every given point one can see the codes in their various intersections. Barthes identifies five codes in particular. They mark out the specific zones which divide up a text into a "broken or obliterated network" of cultural voices, and in these different textual zones we can recognize the encoded potentiality of narrative structure as discussed in chapters 3 and 4. The five codes are:

1 the *proairetic* code, which provides the basis of events and sequences, proliferating linearly and irreversibly;
2 the *semic* code, which provides the basis of character traits;
3 the *hermeneutic* code, which provides the basis of a macrostructure linearly and irreversibly directed towards closure;

4  the *symbolic* code, which provides the basis of representation through reversible binary oppositions;

5  the *reference* code, which provides the basis of seemingly extra-textual referentiality.

The point of isolating these five codes is not to put them together so that they work harmoniously in a whole and finite structure, but to break them apart and keep them separated "in order to observe therein the migration of meanings, the outcroppings of codes, the passages of citations" (Barthes 1974: 14).

## The proairetic code

The proairetic code gives a narrative its potential to organize a story as a linear sequencing of events occurring in time. This code marks signifiers of action and then groups them in a sequence according to the signified of the effect they produce: "since these actions produce effects, each effect will have a generic name giving a kind of title to the sequence . . . the sequence exists when and because it can be given a name, it unfolds as this process of naming takes place" (Barthes 1974: 18–19). The proairetic code "principally determines the readability of the text" (262) and is the basis of structural analysis. However, because the proairetic code only connotes sequences (i.e. it names recognizable actions and their effects), "its only logic is that of the 'already-done' or 'already-read'" (19); so it does not distinguish between the kernel or satellite status of events, nor does it combine microsequences together in macro-sequences to form a macrostructure. Rather, it delimits a textual zone of discrete and multiple sequences: sets of actions that begin and end, continue and stop in time. In fact, since a narrative consists of so much proairetic encoding of simple linear temporality, this code can easily conceal an ellipsis, allowing an event that is not narrated to be inferred from its effect.

The proairetic code, then, distributes events in sequence only as a succession of effects (i.e. Elizabeth must dress and leave her home before she can enter the drawing-room at Netherfield, she must enter before she can look for Wickham, etc.). The difficulty we noted in chapter 3 of absolutely distinguishing between an event and a succession of events (as in the case of Elizabeth's entrance at the Netherfield dance) occurs because a narrative always encodes more proairetic activity than it can organize into a macrostructure. For example, when summarizing the story of *Pride and Prejudice* in chapter 3, we listed fifteen kernel events. The text proairetically encodes these as a series of multiple actions grouped together in sequences under the name of their effect (e.g. meeting, insulting, disliking, etc.). Our summary thus included only what we considered to be the most important events in the story, and those listed events are actually the names of complex proairetic sequences.

## The semic code

While all codes arise from and govern connotations, the semic code inscribes the field where signifiers point to other signifiers to produce the chain of recognizable connotations, as in the word "mourning" from the *Bleak House* passage. A seme is the particular semantic unit of connotation, the sign functioning most obviously as "a shifting element" which produces "flickers of meaning" (Barthes 1974: 17, 19). We have already defined this code, albeit indirectly, in our discussion of traits in chapter 3. Barthes explains the relation of seme to character in this way:

> The seme (or the signified of connotation, strictly speaking) is a connotator of persons, places, objects, of which the signified is a *character*. Character is an adjective, an attribute, a predicate (for example: *unnatural, shadowy, star, opposite, excessive, impious*, etc.). Even though the connotation may be clear, the nomination of its signified is uncertain, approximate, unstable. . . . The seme is only a *departure*, an avenue of meaning. (Barthes 1974: 190–1)

The semic code marks character as a succession of semantic effects, which can be generically named as a trait. For example, the name of Lydia Bennet's elopement is "reckless." Since "semes can migrate from one figure in the text to another" (191), however, this code does not actually individualize character – as we explained in chapter 3, characters can share traits – but inscribes a textual zone of characterization through traiting.

The semic code lays out the unstructured textual materials

of character in much the same way that the proairetic code unfolds the unstructured textual material of story. While the proairetic encodes actions, the minimal units of a story, the semic encodes traits, the minimal units of character. And, while the proairetic groups events in a sequence that can be generically named according to the effect which the events produce as their collective signified, the semic repeats "identical semes [which] traverse the same proper name several times and appear to settle upon it" (Barthes 1974: 67) as a generic characteristic of a semic grouping (such as reckless, talkative, arrogant, etc.).

For example, in one of the stories from James Joyce's *Dubliners*, when Eveline sees her boyfriend Frank for the first time, "he was standing at the gate, his peaked cap pushed back on his head and his hair tumbled forward over a face of bronze" (Joyce 1962: 38–9). Each of these signifiers connotes a signified of Frank's appearance: "standing" (his position at the gate), "peaked" and "pushed back" (the angle of his cap), "tumbled" (his hair), "bronze" (the color of his face). The semic encoding of this description, however, does not stop here. "Bronze" signifies not only a brownish-gold color but also a metal, so, even as the word semically encodes tanned, healthy, sexy, it also encodes medallion or statue or idol, something valued, even worshipped. These various signifieds of "bronze" in turn connote attractive manliness because they encode associations of a bronzed face with the kind of masculinity valued by our culture and depicted by the Marlboro man or Calvin Klein male models in advertisements.

"Bronze" is a word that is "already read" in that its presence as a signifier in this text is overlaid with one's recognition of its presence elsewhere in other (literary and non-literary) texts. To block out these intertextual associations, in an effort to read this text in isolation from other ones, would consequently empty the word "bronze" of its semantic potential; for this signifier marks out in Joyce's text merely a space for connotation. One can say the same about the other, more apparently concrete words which make up this description too. Connoting the rakish or alluring way Frank stands and wears his hat, "tumbled," "peaked," and "standing" lead to the same signified as "bronze," and by way of the same type of cultural associations.

The description as a whole characterizes Frank by encoding a semic field of connotation for that proper name, the effects of which are generically named "virility."

## The hermeneutic code

Put most simply, the hermeneutic is the code of narrative suspense. It determines a particular expectation of narrative on the part of the reader, for it raises, as the overarching premise of narrative, the basic question: what will happen next in the story and why? This is the code which most readers look for, in story after story, to find the ground of meaning for events and characters. Its emphasis in a given text will encourage the practice of reading only "for the story," just as that reading practice will attend to this code over others regardless of its emphasis (or lack of) in a given text.

Marking "all the units whose function it is to articulate in various ways a question, its response, and the variety of chance events which can either formulate or delay its answer; or even, constitute an enigma and lead to its solution" (Barthes 1974: 17), the hermeneutic code filters the proairetic and semic "noise" of a text. Barthes compares the operation of the hermeneutic code to the way in which rhyme and meter structure verse through the repetition of sound and cadence (respectively). Through the repetition of an enigma – a signifier whose signified is disturbingly suppressed by the narration – the hermeneutic code linearly and irreversibly organizes the proairetic encoding of events into a macrostructured story. Similarly, the hermeneutic code can locate the semic encoding of traits in a stable characterization by linking the promise of solution with the revelation of motives.

The hermeneutic enigma can be posed as an obvious mystery, as in the opening of the film *The Letter* when Leslie shoots Hammond; or it can be posed as an explicit question that needs to be answered, as in the *Cathy* comic strip; or it can be posed more complexly and implicitly, as in the many mistakes and secrets which riddle *Pride and Prejudice* because of Darcy and Wickham's past relations. Whatever its particular guise, this code "structure[s] the enigma according to the expectation and desire for its solution"; but in order "to *maintain* the enigma in the initial void of its answer," the code also "must set up _delays_ (obstacles, stoppages, deviations) in the flow of the discourse" (Barthes 1974: 75). This code, in other words, raises an enigma only to keep increasing its narratological value by delaying or obscuring revelations. Such postponement, in turn, structures the desire to read for the end, for the disclosure that will occur in the story's closure as the ultimate signified of both story and character. In this way the hermeneutic code imposes over the temporal sequencing of events the narrative structure of place-ment/displacement/replacement, which it directs towards a particular goal: the point in which the story's transformation of question into answer encodes the answer with "the basic condition for truth" (76).

## The symbolic code

The symbolic code is the most complex and abstrusely defined of the codes in S/Z, and yet, along with the reference code, it is the most central to the intepretation of texts. For, unlike the other three codes, the symbolic is the one that marks out the textual zone of representation. Here, as the name of this code attests, one sign stands in for – and so represents – another.

The symbolic code represents meaning as difference (this sign but not that one). This code marks out "the province of the antithesis" (Barthes 1974: 17) – a "*given* opposition" (27) such as male/female, good/evil – as the field in which culture articu-lates meaning by representing it differentially through symbolic identities so that the opposition appears inevitable and non-linguistic. The function of antithesis "is to consecrate (and domesticate) . . . the division between opposites and the very irreducibility of this division. . . . Every joining of two antithet-ical terms, every mixture, every conciliation – in short, every passage through the wall of the Antithesis – thus constitutes a transgression" (26–7). In its articulation of difference – the slash mark between opposites that identifies them as distinct signs – the symbolic code not only separates but also joins, so it allows for the transgression as well as the conservation of the binaries through which culture identifies, privileges, and naturalizes its representations of symbolic value.

The signifying relations arranged by metaphor and metonymy, as analyzed in chapter 2, symbolically encode meaning differentially; so do the homologous binary oppositions that underlie event and character, as analyzed in chapter 3. And as we showed in those discussions, since difference is simply a reversible opposition, the symbolic code fixes meanings through difference and at the same time unfixes them through difference.

Narratives often place the symbolic code in conjunction with the hermeneutic code, thereby stabilizing its play of difference in order to reproduce and keep in place certain cultural representations of meaning. We illustrated such a collaboration when we discussed how the pairing of the binaries marry/remain single and court/elope encodes Elizabeth and Darcy's marriage symbolically so that it represents the union of moral, gendered, and social oppositions. It is therefore important to distinguish the symbolic code from the hermeneutic; for it is the latter code which fixes in place Elizabeth and Darcy's union as a symbol of reconciliation by aligning it to the story's closure, where the enigma is resolved to effect a claim of truth for the story's ending. By contrast, unlike the hermeneutic code (and more like the semic), the symbolic code traces a textual zone of "multivalence and . . . reversibility; the main task is always to demonstrate that this field can be entered from any number of points, thereby making depth and secrecy problematic" (Barthes 1974: 19). This field of symbolically encoded representation exceeds the stability of irreversible hermeneutic closure, as we also illustrated in chapter 3 when we discussed how a story's paradigmatic structure can resolve the binary oppositions it raises only by suppressing terms of difference.

The symbolic code inscribes the text as a site in which the privileging of one binary term over another is both staged and exposed, legitimized and placed in jeopardy. Barthes himself defines this symbolic site in what he calls "phallic terms" (Barthes 1974: 35), his point being that sexual opposition is the primary way in which our culture represents identity.

The "phallus," as Barthes uses the term, following the psychoanalyst Jacques Lacan, is not literally the penis but, rather, the patriarchical signifier of power, fullness, the law. The symbolic field distributes identities along an axis of gender based on the presence or absence of the phallus. "Male" symbolizes having the phallus – or being plenitude – the

meaningful sign of gendered identity, while "female" symbolizes not having the phallus or being lack.[1] Against these "two
opposing terms" are set "a mixed, and a neuter" (Barthes 1974:
35). "Androgyny" symbolizes the simultaneous presence of
having and lacking (i.e. the androgyne has both the male's plenitude and the female's lack), while "castration" symbolizes the
simultaneous negation of having and lacking (i.e. the eunuch
has a penis but lacks the phallus). The two opposing terms
stabilize the representation of sexual difference around the
signifier of the phallus as irreducibly "masculine" and "feminine." The mixed and neuter terms, on the other hand, transgress – "scandalize," as Barthes also puts it – the representation
of sexual difference, with "androgyny" exceeding it, "castration" emptying it. By locating "male" and "female" in culture,
not biology, the symbolic code repeatedly threatens to collapse
the difference that enables those two opposing terms to mean by
referring, not to the symbolic order of culture, but to nature.
The symbolic code therefore reproduces but also just as easily
disturbs the apparently natural order of sexual difference.

As set forth in this way, the symbolic coding of sexual
difference is not unique to a given text but, on the contrary, is
the reproduction of a culturally signifying field in which "man"
means "humankind" or "person" and "woman" means
"female person" or "not a man." The symbolic encoding of
even these opposing terms, however, disrupts their cultural
meanings by displacing signifieds from signifiers. Since the
semic field of character traiting is itself not a stable or consistent
one, characters can occupy positions in this symbolic field
regardless of their semically encoded biological gender. The
symbolic code jeopardizes the stability of cultural meanings
whenever it lets slip "the paradigmatic slash mark which
permits meaning to function" (Barthes 1974: 215) – and which,
in its representation of antithesis (i.e. male/female), also puts
the lie to the hermeneutical truth of a text's full and final
disclosure of a meaning.

One of the primary symbolic codes of *Dracula*, for example,
is male/female, which the text represents in the phallic terms
described above by differentiating gender, as in the figures of
Lucy Westenra and her three suitors, on the basis of having/
lacking. All the same, the text can assert the importance of that

symbolic opposition only by representing its perversion in the androgynous figure of Dracula. He has blood-red lips and long fingernails; and while he is the one who usually sucks blood from the neck of his victims for nourishment, and is said to have a child's brain, at one point he nurses Mina Harker on blood from a vein opened at his "bare breast," "forcing her face down on his bosom" (Stoker 1965: 288). Likewise, his victim Mina can be read as a castrated figure when she is described as if she were a man lacking. She is said to have "man's brain – a brain that a man should have were he much gifted – and a woman's heart" (Stoker 1965: 241), that is, she has the brain with the power of a man but in a female body. The importance of these two deviations of the male/female difference is twofold. First, it shows that the symbolic field exceeds biological difference. Female characters can be encoded as masculine, and masculine characters can be encoded as feminine. Second, and as a result, the symbolic encoding of Dracula and Mina shows how the gendered differences which represent meaning to a culture can be, and often are, transgressed or collapsed entirely.

Dracula, in fact, is symbolically encoded to represent the articulation of a number of differences: just as he is male and female, he is dead and alive, old and young, mother and child. Dracula, then, symbolizes pure difference: he is the demonic Other to every cultural meaning which the text cites. The symbolic threat which Dracula represents is only eliminated with his destruction in the name of good over evil, spirituality over profanity, salvation over damnation, nature over the supernatural, day over night, reason over madness. The symbolic mixture of female and male in Mina, on the other hand, is never as problematic because she serves the dominant white, patriarchal, western, and Christian society which defines itself in opposition to Dracula; and at the end of the story she is refeminized by bearing a child, another male. The oppositions in the symbolic code of this text, then, are at once rigidly defined, challenged and perverted, and reinstated when the text joins that code to the hermeneutic.

## The reference code

The reference code supplies a text with an assortment of "references to a science or body of knowledge" (Barthes 1974:

20), which, "taken up from citation to citation, together form an oddly joined miniature version of encyclopedic knowledge" (184–5). Such references reproduce a very familiar reality because they quote from the large assortment of social texts which mediate and organize cultural knowledge about reality: medicine, law, religion, morality, psychology, history, science, literature, philosophy, not to mention all the clichés and proverbs of popular culture. The reference code is thus a general category of the many culture codes which speak through us and to us whenever we use language. As its name implies, its function is to provide a text with cultural frames of reference: a heterogeneous mix of intertextual citations to the already said, the maxims of truth circulating through a culture and accepted as the given knowledge of common sense.

Many contemporary "postmodern" narratives make such mediation of the text very explicit by over-encoding cultural references. *Heartbreak Tango*, for example, includes frequent references to North and South American popular culture (films, soap opera, romances, magazines, beauty, clothing, songs, dances, superstitions), as well as to religion, class, ethnicity, gender, family, love, and so on. Subtitled "A Serial" in the manner of soap operas, *Heartbreak Tango* consists of numbered episodes, each bearing an epigraph from a song, a movie ad, or a radio commercial. At times the text takes the form of social documents – the obituary or society pages of a newspaper, an advice column in a magazine, police and hospital reports. The language of these documents is a collage of phrasings that do not originate with the individual who utters them but circulate in society as maxims or commonplace truths. "The charming Nélida Fernández," one columnist writes, has a "svelte figure"; when she dances with Juan Carlos, the pair "convincingly demonstrated the age-old adage 'Love makes the world go round,' as Mrs Baños declared" (Puig 1981: 19). The characters' narrations – in letters, memo books, or stream-of-consciousness monologues – similarly draw upon the numerous and not always compatible codes of their culture, to religion and popular music, to class and Hollywood films.

Although an encoding of heterogeneous cultural references is taken to typify avant-garde narratives, we suspect that it stands out in a text like *Heartbreak Tango* only because the codes it quotes, dominating western culture at this historical moment, are very familiar to us as codes. Even so, the culture codes we can most easily recognize in *Heartbreak Tango* are those which the text appropriates from Anglo-American culture and not the ones which Latin American readers would recognize from their own culture (specific codes of politics, history, family, church, gender). Made up of codes that are culturally and historically specific, a text's referentiality may therefore go unnoticed as coding.

To contemporary readers, older and more realistic narratives like *Pride and Prejudice* or *Bleak House* may appear not to be quoting culture codes at all. Those narratives nevertheless rely just as much on a strong and heterogeneous reference code, and they do so specifically to authenticate their claims of representing a fictional world that is "true to life." The short *Bleak House* passage, analyzed in chapter 2, draws heavily upon culture codes of law, economics, science, mourning, and industrialism in order to give the impression of a particular, localized geography which conveys a sense of "real" Victorian London. "The imaginary London of *Bleak House*," Terry Eagleton explains, "exists as the product of a representational process which signifies, not 'Victorian England' as such, but certain of Victorian England's ways of signifying itself" (Eagleton 1978: 77). The various culture codes of this text interact with each other to provide one version of the real which Victorian England claimed as "true," and to which the text refers in signifying London.

More so than the other four codes, the reference code marks out an intertextual zone in which culture mediates subjective knowledge of reality through its many codes. The advertisement, as we pointed out, turns the symbolic field of quality into "a natural reference, into a proverbial statement" (Barthes 1974: 98), by overlaying it with the reference codes of the signature label and nature. Invading every text in one form or another, the reference code appears most prominently when, as in *Heartbreak Tango*, a text cites truisms, proverbs, and clichés, those referent systems which originate in the collective and anonymous voice of society as a kind of automatic speech. In *Brighton Rock* Ida Arnold repeatedly quotes truisms about justice, and we are told that her aphorisms "came clicking out like

a ticket from a slot machine" (Greene 1977: 199). The quotation
of maxims in this text is not limited to Ida's own speeches; the
narration also cites them when describing her: "Man is made by
the places in which he lives, and Ida's mind worked with the
simplicity and the regularity of a skysign" (37). The narration
encodes references to other stereotypical bodies of knowledge as
well – class, gender, religion – and these are no different from
Ida's aphorisms about justice. Less apparent as stereotypical
knowledge, they may appear more naturalized as "truths." But
when the narration comments, "She was of the people, she cried
in cinemas at *David Copperfield*" (32), it actually characterizes
Ida through a code of class, referring to a social stereotype about
the vulgar sentimentality of "the people," i.e. the working and
not the middle class.

   Referentially encoded meanings seem inevitable and uncontestable, only because – and when – they are instantly recognizable as (cultural) truths. Culture codes, however, are subject to
history. Readers thus read texts differently at different historical
moments because the same culture codes are not always available as intertextual frames of reference. The opening paragraph
of *Bleak House* signifies the time of year (November) through
the code of the law (Michaelmas Term), and contemporary
American readers may miss this reference, although Victorian
readers would surely not have. While referential meanings from
past cultures may be uncovered – from a dictionary like the
*Oxford English Dictionary* – they are never fully recoverable
because they are always mediated by a contemporary reader's
culture and its codes. This is why Frank's "face of bronze,"
discussed above, cannot be read innocently by a 1980s reader,
i.e. as if all the bronzed faces in magazines and television ads do
not interfere with the reading of Joyce's text today. A text's
signifiers remain the same, of course, but their signifieds change
because culture codes change; as a result, the specificity of a
text's cultural references alters, even to the point of
disappearing entirely.

   In our discussion of the five codes we have mentioned story
several times but not narration. We could easily add a sixth code
of communication solely responsible for the telling of a story (as
Barthes himself did in an essay on codes written after *S/Z*[2]).
Narration, however, cannot be so easily separated from the

numerous and heterogeneous cultural references that comprise a text. For a reader's ability to recognize the communicative features of narration results from the text's encoding of narrative conventions that signify how it means as a telling. We can term this a _diegetic_ code, a code most easily understood with an example from film. In a film one can read emotion in the close-up of an actor's face, notice a detail emphasized by camera movement or lighting, and determine the spatial position of a character or the passage of time through editing, because in each case the shot encodes – refers to – a code of diegesis governing the telling of story in the cinematic medium. This code identifies signifiers of telling (a close-up, say) and links them to a signified (the character's mental life). We can say the same of the various configurations of temporality, agency, and focalization which we discussed in chapter 4; these encompass the diegetic code for the medium of prose narration.

Although the diegetic code seems to differ in kind from the culture coding of a text, it is also part of the reference code. It draws upon socially acquired and historically determined knowledge of how one medium means as opposed to any other. Diegetic references, moreover, never appear independently of references to other culture codes. As an example, recall passage 10 in the previous chapter, the description of Robert Crosbie in Somerset Maugham's short story "The Letter." Robert is large, muscular, hirsute, sunburnt from supervising the estate and from playing tennis. The semic and symbolic encoding of this passage sets up a play of connotation (virility) and phallic antithesis (strong/weak, light/dark, etc.) which the references to class, gender, and race momentarily fix in place. The diegetic coding of this description presents the cultural values of upper-class, male, white domination as a physical and natural fact about Robert; it then attributes, through figural focalization, the observation of this fact to the personal insight of a character, Mr Joyce. In doing so, the diegesis simply encodes another social truth, that the kind of value Robert represents originates in individuality, in personal insight, and not in culture.

Segmenting a text according to these five codes opens up the scope of textual analysis so that it can address cultural practices of signification (which is what the text, finally, is encoding). Each of the five codes, Barthes comments,

> is one of the forces that can take over the text (of which the text is the network), one of the voices out of which the text is woven. Alongside each utterance, one might say that off-stage voices can be heard: they are the codes: in their interweaving, these voices (whose origin is "lost" in the vast perspective of the *already-written*) de-originate the utterance. (Barthes 1974: 21)

Quoting the "already-written," these multiple "off-stage" voices reiterate cultural assumptions about the capacity of narrative (or any text, really) to mean: that actions are sequential, their logic inducible from their effect (the proairetic); that people are the autonomous sum of innate features (the semic); that a story conceals a secret, the disclosure of which amounts to closure (the hermeneutic); that symbols represent uncontestable and inevitable meanings (the symbolic); that reality transcends textuality (the reference). The codes succeed when they appear to trace a course of meanings originating in the text and not the course by which culture supplies meaning for the signs comprising that text.

At issue when analyzing a text's codes is not the recovery of an "original" meaning but the dissemination of meanings. A multiply encoded text, as Williamson points out about advertisements and Barthes about narrative, draws upon many different referent systems, translating between them to "constitute a vast meta-system where values from different areas of our lives are made interchangeable" (Williamson 1978: 25). Codes make the reading of signs appear effortless so long as they do not impede the progression from one referent system to another. The ease with which systems of meaning can be interchanged – for instance, the way the signifieds of nature automatically become signifiers of Woolrich products – silences the text's noise as a plural signifying field. Decoding a text, on the other hand, attends to its noise so as to analyze how, at any given lexia, codes facilitate or block the exchange of signs necessary for the production of meaning. Further, with a text being traversed and striated by *multiple* codes, decoding exposes the contradictions in cultural meanings which result from the text's heterogeneity.

## Decoding cultural meanings

The origin of a text's many voices, as Barthes says, is "lost" because, in transmitting cultural meanings, codes locate signification in *ideology*.[3] Ideology is a somewhat difficult term to define because it is primarily evident through its effects. That is, ideology promotes ideas and beliefs which seem true or natural as the result of reasonable, commonsensical observation. We are not saying that ideology obscures more real or valid ideas and beliefs in the name of a false doctrine, or that there are some ideas and beliefs which are free of ideology as opposed to those which are not. Rather, ideology amounts to "the sum of the ways in which people both live and represent to themselves their relationship to the conditions of their existence" (Belsey 1980: 42). Such representations operate in culture as the medium through which "human beings live their lives as conscious actors in a world that makes sense to them to varying degrees" (Therborn 1980: 2). Viewed in this light, ideology is not a system of true or false beliefs and values, a doctrine, so much as it is the means by which culture represents beliefs and values. And, just as culture is not monolithic or homogeneous, neither is ideology. As Louis Althusser explains, "an ideology is a system (with its own logic and rigour) of representations (images, myths, ideas or concepts, depending on the case) endowed with a historical existence and role within a given society" (Althusser 1977: 231).

We can thus define ideology as a medium of symbolic representations depicting the values and beliefs according to which people live out their lives in the social structure they inhabit.[4] A system of representation, ideology is real and material. However, what an ideology represents is "not the system of the real relations which govern the existence of individuals, but the imaginary relation of those individuals to the real relations in which they live" (Althusser 1971: 165). Providing the "real" enabling conditions of knowledge and action, ideologies are, at the same time, "imaginary" – in the double sense of fabricating and imaging – because they are the representations of meaning that mediate all knowledge and action. Silencing contradiction and evading alternative representations of the real, an ideology represents society's network of power relations as inevitable and natural, beyond question or change. Bourgeois ideology, for instance, glosses over or fully evades the divisions of race, gender, and class that empower the cultural values and beliefs motivating people's lives. Instead it depicts these relations in terms of comforting verities – Happiness, Fairness, Motherhood, Noble Suffering, etc.

The Woolrich ad offers a relatively simple example of an ideological representation. It treats leisure time as if it were constant, available to everyone, and always fun. And, in so doing, the ad masks reality – it does not lie but it is highly selective in its encoding of the conditions which motivate the need for Woolrich products. The ad does not suggest that cold temperatures might require jackets and coats for reasons other than leisure activities. It omits mention of labor practices as well as the workers who cannot afford Woolrich. It also excludes single people, or non-Caucasians, homosexuals, and multiracial couples.

Key differences in the ad's encoding of pleasure and class expose what it must gloss over in order to equate Happiness with Status. 1890s prosperity is semically encoded by a white family, while that of the 1980s by a white but also young, heterosexual, upwardly mobile, childless couple. Also, while 1890s leisure is proairetically encoded in terms of sledding – an action – the contemporary picture encodes leisure as passive. The 1980s couple poses for a picture, and, while there is a ski rack on their car, there is not even any snow for skiing. Superimposed upon the old, grainy black-and-white photograph, which images active, outdoor pleasure, the glossy new photograph is more heavily invested in signifying that the way to get a purchase on Happiness is through class standing. The ad therefore equates Happiness, which it depicts as a natural drive, with Status, a socially constructed category.

If we examine the ad's superimposition of one picture on another more closely, we can also see how this ideological representation of Happiness and Status circumvents the problem of history while in the very act of raising it. Together, these two photos symbolize generational continuity, encoding the message: what was good enough for your grandparents is good enough for you. The choice of the word "folks" for people of the 1890s referentially encodes universality – common, ordinary, unpretentious people. Furthermore, the dates in the copy include two numbers (8 and 9) that are just one digit apart in our counting system and signify sameness by their ability to shift position. Despite this insistence on sameness, the superimposition of photographs symbolically encodes a historical difference between the two eras which the ad tries to reconcile through a reference code of nostalgia. Whereas the ad tells a linear narrative pointing out the resemblance between two generations separated in time, the ad pictures this relation as based solely on contiguity, the placement of one photograph next to another. The visual narration, then, makes a metaphor out of a metonymy. Drawing on the reference code of the new in the shiny, expensive car and the technological enhancement of the contemporary photo, the visual narration indicates that things do change over time, which contradicts the verbal narration's encoding of history as memory – as nostalgia and tradition.

Ideology makes itself most visible when texts like advertisements represent value as originating naturally and not culturally. Such articulations of "natural" value, as we showed in our discussion of codes, are by no means limited to ads. Ideology is encoded in language use – in discourse – where it fixes the play of signifiers by authorizing certain signifieds. The referent system of a code, in other words, is an ideological system regulating the terms of representation (one sign standing in for another), for the individuals using the signs either to send or to receive meanings. As Williamson comments:

> A sign replaces something for someone. It can only mean if it has someone to mean *to*. Therefore, all signs depend for their signifying process on the existence of specific, concrete receivers, people *for* whom, and in whose systems of belief, they have a meaning. Moreover, signs are only signs in their actual *process* of replacing something; in other words, being exchanged with it *by* a particular person or people. It is in the dialectic between the "for" and the "by" that ideology maintains its momentum. (Williamson 1978: 40)

For this reason, ideology must be understood as real and material, determining the politics of what signs mean and to/for whom, and deeply complicit in discursive enunciations of subjectivity: "All ideology," Althusser maintains, "has the function (which defines it) of 'constituting' concrete individuals as subjects" (Althusser 1971: 171).

This is a difficult concept, but before we explain it the term *subject* needs further comment. We have talked about the "subject" of events (in chapter 3) and the "subject" in discourse (in chapter 4). In doing so we have used the term *subject* to signify an individual (1) who performs an action – doing, thinking, feeling; (2) who apprehends him- or herself as an identifiable agent of action, the grammatical subject of a predication; and (3) who finds a signifier of that identity in discourse, *I* as opposed to *you*. But *subject* is also a term of passivity, as when one is subject to a monarch or law, or the subject of an experiment. Falling within these two poles of agency and passivity, *subjectivity* is the condition of being (a) subject. The role of ideology in constituting the subject is to keep reiterating that parenthetical "a" so that the individual feels whole, individuated, and responsible for meaning in the face of his or her subjection to cultural representations of meaning.

Ideology, that is to say, represents subjectivity as a state of continuous self-apprehension – of being an acting, thinking, and feeling subject (an "I") – in order to subject the individual to meanings that perpetuate the social structure. Althusser describes such subjection occurring through the ideological "hailing" of individuals as subjects – the subjects, we hasten to add, of a discourse.

> ideology "acts" or "functions" in such a way that it "recruits" subjects among the individuals (it recruits them all), or "transforms" the individuals into subjects (it transforms them all) by that very precise operation which I have called *interpellation* or hailing, and which can be imagined along the lines of the most commonplace everyday police (or other) hailing: "Hey, you there!" (Althusser 1971: 174)

We have already explained how language use establishes the linguistic conditions of subjectivity. Because *you* always implies its opposite *I*, hailing induces self-recognition on the part of the subject being addressed: "Yes, that's me!"

In narrative, focalization can serve as a powerful inducement of interpellation, which is why we stressed that the diegetic code is another culture code. Narration sets forth an ideological address that positions the reading subject in relation to discourse. In the description of Leslie from Somerset Maugham's short story "The Letter" (passage 11 in chapter 4), "you" are hailed as her observer; and, as you identify with the signifier *you*, you not only find an ideological representation of femininity semically and symbolically encoded in this passage, but you also find your subjectivity in that representation. Such hailing is not limited to instances of direct address. As we stated in chapter 4, the subject of narration functions as a signifier of the subject bespoken by that narration. Thus the other two passages we quoted from this story also interpellate you to ideological representations of the Orient (passage 9) and of masculinity (passage 10).

The Woolrich ad likewise reiterates an ideological representation of Happiness and Status for you, the reader whom it addresses as the interpellated subject of this equation: if you buy Woolrich products, not only will you feel pleasure, but you will acquire status and take pleasure in your class standing. This message is contradictory but reassuring; in assenting to its logic you differentiate yourself from people who do not buy Woolrich. You identify, that is, with people like the couple in the picture, and as this happens the ad represents your subjectivity to you in the form of a signifier of pleasurable Status. In other words, the ad produces a "natural" articulation of values that depends on your being hailed as subject of that articulation. Identifying with the subject of the ad, you become its signified the very moment you make it mean. This is how ideology retains its power as a real medium of imaginary understanding: it makes you the subject *of* as well as *to* its representation of meaning. As this interpellation occurs, "ideology produces the individual in a relation to a representation within the social process in which he or she is situated, as an *identity* (a point of self-reference) rather than a *process*" (Coward and Ellis 1977: 77; our italics).

What we are saying applies just as much to the speaking (and

writing) subject of discourse. As with the enunciation of subjectivity occurring in the hailing of *you*, the articulation of *I* involves
a process of self-enunciation that appears to confirm identity as
an autonomous and continuous point of self-reference. But the
pronoun *I*, we explained in chapter 4, does not refer to an
individual speaker so much as it points elsewhere in the utterance for an antecedent. In doing that, the subject of speech *I*
makes the speaker subject to speech, to the cultural meanings
encoded in the signs comprising the utterance, so the signifier of
identity which the speaker finds in his or her own discourse is
also an ideological representation of subjectivity. Bespoken by
discourse, subjectivity occurs as the result of this process of
self-recognition, which is repeatedly activated every time a
speaker uses language. Only by concealing this process can
ideology induce in the speaker the misrecognition of subjectivity
as an extra-discursive, continuous identity. And, so long as the
discursive production of subjectivity is kept concealed, the
meanings to which the individual finds him- or herself subject to
when using language appear to fall outside of signification – and
beyond change or intervention.[5]

When Althusser attributes the seeming naturalness of understanding to the subject's interpellation by an ideological representation (as in our examples of the Woolrich ad and "The
Letter"), he is arguing that the subject grasps him- or herself as
unified and coherent – in possession not only of truth but also of
subjectivity – at the very moment he or she grasps meaning.
Althusser's explanation of the relation between ideology and
subjectivity, however, does not take full account of the division
of subjectivity that occurs in discourse, the heterogeneous
encoding of utterances, and the multiplicity of utterances char-
acterizing language use. Just as ideology is always more than
mere ideas, the subject spoken by ideology is more than a
container or empty space filled up by those ideas. The subject is
never truly whole or coherent in spite of interpellation: this very
incompleteness is why ideology must repeatedly (re)constitute
the subject in discourse.

More to the point, ideology is plural, and so is the subject it
speaks. Culture promotes different ideologies which represent
the subject differently, so, while an ideology marks out the
signifiers which position the subject of speech in discourse, it

cannot ensure the continuity or stability of the subject through signification. Although the effect of an ideology, as we have said, is to provide such assurance, the subject actually grasps him- or herself from across a full range of ideologically conflicting discourses.

In order to address this last point, we need to extend our understanding of *discourse* beyond that advanced in the previous chapter, where we used the term to designate language practices in general. Discourse is, as Michel Foucault has argued, a much less politically neutral term than our previous use may have implied. Any given discourse has a social materiality and ideological particularity that differentiates it from other discourses according to the conditions of its formation and practice.

For Foucault, *discourse* is more than simply the "general domain of all statements" (Foucault 1972: 80) – the realization in speech (*parole*) of a language system (*langue*). Rather, he points out, discourse is "an individualizable group of statements" (80) which can be recognized as a group because they are all part of the same *discursive formation*:

> We shall call discourse a group of statements in so far as they belong to the same discursive formation; it does not form a rhetorical or formal unity, endlessly repeatable, whose appearance or use in history might be indicated (and, if necessary, explained); it is made up of a limited number of statements for which a group of conditions of existence can be defined. (Foucault 1972: 117)

A discourse can be analyzed according to the linguistic rules governing all the utterances of a language but also, and more pointedly, in terms of the specific formation that groups the enunciation of statements similar in kind. As well as being governed by a particular formation, Foucault continues, a discourse is the result of "a regulated practice that accounts for a certain number of statements" (80). A *discursive practice* regulates the enunciation of statements by imposing "a body of anonymous, historical rules, always determined in the time and space that have defined a given period, and for a given social, economic, geographical, or linguistic area, the conditions of operation of the enunciative function" (117). Though there is a plurality of discourses at any given time, a single discourse is limited *to* the finite number of possible statements which characterize it as a formation, and it is limited *by* the historical and social conditions in which it is practiced, the "body of anonymous, historical rules" allowing for the combination of one discourse with others but also differentiating one discourse from others.

Medical discourse, for example, which became considerably enlarged after the founding of the clinic in the late eighteenth century, can be easily studied in these terms. It is located in institutions (hospitals, clinics, public health offices, etc.) and in practices (the performances of operations, lab testing for illness, therapies, etc.); and it is composed of certain kinds of statements which take specific rhetorical forms, such as hypotheses, diagnoses, prognoses, prescriptions. Within these forms, specialized vocabulary narrows the discourse further: drugs have specific generic as well as brand names which must be mastered before a prescription can be drawn up; mental illnesses are coded by a medical handbook and are so written by the doctor on a patient's insurance claims; the condition of hospitalized patients is gradated as "serious," "critical," "stable," "improving"; and so on. Furthermore, those empowered to use medical discourse – doctors, nurses, private or public health officials, medical students, pharmacists – are awarded the right to do so only after training in specialized medical programs that certify them as experts. Able to practice only at certain times under certain conditions and at certain locations, these experts control the practice of the discourse through which the profession excludes or, at best, marginalizes competing practices of health care: acupuncture, say, or holistic medicine, or midwifery.[6]

Although professions define themselves in their discursive practices, discourses are by no means limited to the professions. The Woolrich ad referentially encodes a discourse of class – the "yuppie" discourse of the American post-World War II baby boom – which can be described in the same terms as medical discourse. This discourse is a formation of late twentieth-century capitalism; it is made visible in social practices – white-collar employment, regulated leisure, consumption – which govern sets of verbal and visual statements such as the

Woolrich ad; and it empowers a certain kind of subject through exclusions based on age and economics.

Throughout his investigations of "the different modes by which, in our culture, human beings are made subjects" (Foucault 1983: 208), Foucault analyzes how a particular discursive complex of statement, formation, and practice constitutes subjectivity in relation to power and knowledge. Knowledge, he demonstrates, is regulated (and, we are arguing, ideology is perpetuated) to a large degree by the discursive formations of social institutions (such as the medical or yuppie establishment). The knowing subject is subjected to a discourse that shows the *effects* of power in its dissemination of knowledge as truth. Indeed, Foucault goes so far as to claim that discursive practices of institutions actually take primacy over knowledge by making knowledges possible – which is to say that they mark out the boundaries of knowledge for the subject. In regulating what is sayable, how it can be articulated, who can speak, where, and under what conditions, a discursive practice controls the dissemination of certain knowledges, thereby ensuring the domination of certain social interests by producing a certain kind of subject.

Neither a discourse nor the subject it articulates is as coherent or fixed as this summary of Foucault's argument may suggest. On the contrary, a discursive formation "enters simultaneously into several fields of relations, in which it does not occupy the same place, or exercise the same function" (Foucault 1972: 159). For instance, medical discourse is invaded by the discourse of law when a doctor writes a prescription, treats a sexually transmitted disease, testifies at a trial as an expert witness, signs a death certificate, or gets sued for malpractice. While a discourse may seem to have obvious connections to one institution, one site of cultural power, it is not limited to that institution, just as a word is not tied to a specific context. The signifying values of words change from one discourse to another and, within a discourse, refer differentially to their locations in other discursive sites. Likewise, what matters is the position which a discourse holds in an institution, and how that discourse functions differently across institutions.

Because any one discourse is never unitary or isolated either from other discourses or from the activities of power in culture, breakdowns in the regulation of knowledge occur over time. To begin with, a single discursive formation only exists as a heterogeneous or "problematic" unity (Foucault 1972: 79); it contains the elements for its own alterations and appropriations because it is always produced and continuing to evolve in relation to other discourses and their practices: establishing interlinkings, bondings, breaks, ruptures, and undiscovered or emerging formations. As a result, a discursive practice does not merely reproduce, it also transforms knowledge. Modifications of what counts as knowledge take place "outside the domain of a discourse (in the forms of production, in social relationships, or in political institutions), inside it (in its techniques for determining its object, in the adjustment and refinement of its concepts, in its accumulation of facts), or to the side of it (in other discursive practices)"; and often changes occur simultaneously on all fronts (Foucault 1977: 200). Since a discourse registers the effects of power upon knowledge and also functions as the site in which knowledge is transformed and power resisted, discursive enunciations of subjectivity inevitably catch the subject of speech in a web of cultural regulations, contradictions, and realignments. And it is in this sense, Foucault maintains, that subjectivities as well as discourses are the products of history.[7]

Following Foucault, we view a text as the site of struggle among various discourses, each instrumental in controlling the production and transmission of ideological representations of the subject. Narrative texts in particular are likely arenas for such struggle because they are structurally organized around the subject of events (in the story) and of narration (in the telling). We can illustrate by returning to the example of *Jane Eyre*. In the previous chapter we explained how that novel's narration divides subjectivity so that, textually, the subject of narration, Jane Eyre, is not a whole and a continuous identity but a series of fragmented subjectivities inscribed in discourse. We can now extend our discussion by looking more closely at some of the particular discourses that comprise the narration of Jane's subjectivity.

The opening of the second chapter after Jane's fight with John Reed exemplifies the text's discursive plurality to the point of excess and incoherence:

I resisted all the way: a new thing for me, and a circumstance which greatly strengthened the bad opinion Bessie and Miss Abbot were disposed to entertain of me. The fact is, I was a trifle beside myself; or rather *out* of myself, as the French would say: I was conscious that a moment's mutiny had already rendered me liable to strange penalties, and, like any other rebel slave, I felt resolved, in my desperation, to go all lengths.

"Hold her arms, Miss Abbot: she's like a mad cat."

"For shame! for shame!" cried the lady's-maid. "What shocking conduct, Miss Eyre, to strike a young gentleman, your benefactress's son! Your young master."

"Master! How is he my master? Am I a servant?"

"No; you are less than a servant, for you do nothing for your keep. There, sit down, and think over your wickedness." (Brontë, *Jane Eyre*, 1971: 9)

Semically, this passage encodes Jane's character as wild, shocking, violent, ungrateful, wicked. Proairetically, it encodes a sequence of resistance and constraint: the child Jane is being held down and carried away by the two servants. Symbolically, it encodes various antitheses: conscious/unconscious, powerful/powerless, consistency/inconsistency, nature/society, freedom/servitude. Hermeneutically, it encodes two enigmas: the indeterminacy of Jane's social and natal status in the Reed household, and the uncertainty raised by her having acted in a "new" and unpredictable way to disturb the order of the household. As a subject of narration, Jane is, textually speaking, a site traversed by these four codes.

Referentially, the passage locates this subject in a variety of discourses. First, the discourse of revolution represents Jane as a mutinous "rebel slave" who has been subjected to cruel tyranny. But a discourse we would now call psychological also represents Jane's subjectivity as a momentary madness: "I was a trifle beside myself," she says, or, put even more strongly, "*out* of myself." Furthermore, Miss Abbot and Bessie the nurse subject Jane to the discourse of nature in calling her a "cat"; and, when they modify "cat" with "mad," they imply that she is not domesticated but a predator. Finally, Jane is also subjected to discourses of class, patriarchy, and morality: John Reed is her master, the women tell her, and she is wicked to strike the young gentleman, who is socially superior.

While these multiple discourses all contribute to the representation of Jane Eyre as a subject of narration, they do not cohere into a unified subjectivity. Cast as an animal, she exhibits a natural instinct to claw back; cast as John Reed's social inferior, she has stepped outside her station. As a girl, she appears to be a natural inferior – physically weak – yet she must be held down by two adults. Further, she is said to be mad and of a lower class, but are madness and an inferior class position the same? And more to the point: is she a slave (she claims she is) or is she a servant (she says she is not, though the women claim she is)?

As such different discourses emerge and retreat in the text, often intersecting each other, they implicate the representation of Jane's subjectivity in multiple and incompatible ideologies. When Jane goes to work for Rochester as the governess of Thornfield, for instance, patriarchal discourses of class and gender define her sense of being an impoverished, plain, and powerless woman.

> I rose; I dressed myself with care: obliged to be plain – for I had no article of attire that was not made with extreme simplicity – I was still by nature solicitous to be neat. It was not my habit to be disregardful of appearance, or careless of the impression I made: on the contrary, I ever wished to look as well as I could, and to please as much as my want of beauty would permit. I sometimes regretted that I was not handsomer: I sometimes wished to have rosy cheeks, a straight nose, and small cherry mouth; I desired to be tall, stately, and finely developed in figure; I felt it a misfortune that I was so little, so pale, and had features so irregular and so marked. And why had I these aspirations and these regrets? It would be difficult to say to myself; yet I had a reason, and a logical, natural reason too. (Brontë 1971: 86)

In order to articulate her complaints to herself, Jane must turn to an alternative discourse, one which can provide "a logical, natural reason" for what she feels.

> It is in vain to say human beings ought to be satisfied with

tranquility: they must have action; and they will make it if they cannot find it. Millions are condemned to a stiller doom than mine, and millions are in silent revolt against their lot. Nobody knows how many rebellions besides political rebellions ferment in the masses of life which people earth. Women are supposed to feel very calm generally: but women feel just as men feel; they need exercise for their faculties, and a field for their efforts as much as their brothers do; they suffer from too rigid a restraint, too absolute a stagnation, precisely as men would suffer; and it is narrowed in their more privileged fellow-creatures to say that they ought to confine themselves to making puddings and knitting stockings, to playing on the piano and embroidering bags. It is thoughtless to condemn them, or laugh at them, if they seek to do more or learn more than custom has pronounced necessary for their sex. (Brontë 1971: 96)

In this passage the discourse of revolution links Jane's subjectivity to an ideological representation of revolt which is historically specific to the time of the novel's production. This is a discourse of subversion, of "political rebellion." Its terms of signification referentially encode the French Revolution and its aftermath (approximately the time of Jane's story), as well as the social unrest in England occurring in the early decades of the nineteenth century – events such as the Luddite attacks on factories and the Peterloo march that resulted in a riot and bloodshed (the time of Jane's telling).

As it appears in *Jane Eyre*, this discourse of revolution takes as its object, not the Bastille or the factory, but the home, where women suffer "in silent revolt." In this replacement of an open and public site of revolt by a contained and private one, *Jane Eyre* typifies the coding of revolutionary discourse in mid-century representations of revolt. There, according to Nancy Armstrong, family scandal or sexual misconduct stands in for (encodes) social rioting or rebellion as a means of defusing social unrest by combining it with the discourse of domesticity. Family members, who can be educated, locked up, or silenced, are more easily contained than mobs of frustrated, angry workers; and the novels of the 1840s almost routinely depict social revolt through a discourse of revolution tied to age or gender, representing the rebel as a young naïve who is misled (like the young Rochester), or as an impassioned female who is "beside herself" with emotion (like the young Jane), or sometimes even as a monster (like Bertha Mason, Rochester's first wife, imprisoned in his attic). This reencoding of revolutionary discourse, however, also ends up implicating domesticity in revolution, its symbolic binary, by depicting the home as the site of both social unrest and its resolution.

Such discursive heterogeneity can, therefore, only result in contradiction. In the passage we just quoted, Jane declares that "Women are supposed to feel very calm generally: but women feel just as men feel." She apprehends herself as a subject of a discourse transcending social divisions based on gender and class, invoking what Cora Kaplan calls a Romantic ideology of unified identity. "In the passage the generic status of 'men' is made truly trans-class and transcultural when linked to 'masses', 'millions' and 'human beings', those larger exclusive terms" (Kaplan 1985: 171). Kaplan points out that this passage, appearing in a novel published in 1847, "on the eve of the second great wave of modern revolution" (171), is "a moment of radical association between political rebellion and gender rebellion" (173). We do not disagree, though we want to emphasize that Jane un-engenders this discourse only to re-engender it, and that as soon as Rochester arrives at Thornfield she reiterates her subjection to the patriarchal discourses of class and gender: "it had a master," she says of the house; "for my part I liked it better" (Brontë 1971: 103). It is simply not possible for Jane to transcend gender and class while speaking in the discourse of hierarchical, patriarchal norms, any more than it is possible for her to rebel while serving, without becoming the subject of clashing ideological interests.

These contradictions are not simply the result of the cognitive difference in Jane's character between youthfulness and maturity. Narrating retrospectively, the adult Jane apprehends herself as a feeling, thinking, or silenced subject much as the younger Jane does – through discourses that enable her to articulate her subjectivity and that subject her to ideological representations of meaning. The adult Jane cannot identify with that younger rebel, that "discord in Gateshead Hall" (Brontë 1971: 12), but instead misrecognizes herself as "a heterogeneous thing . . . a useless thing . . . a noxious thing" (12). Only as the narrator can she personify "Jane Eyre" to account for "*why* I thus suffered; now, at a distance of – I will not say how many years, I see it clearly" (12). When "Jane Rochester" replaces "Jane Eyre" in the ending to signify "perfect concord" (397), she does so as the subject of marriage. As Jane confides, "I have now been married ten years. . . . I hold myself supremely blest – blest beyond what language can express; because I am my husband's life as fully as he is mine. No woman was ever nearer to her mate than I am; ever more absolutely bone of his bone and flesh of his flesh" (396–7). By citing Genesis 2:23, Jane proves that she is hardly as beyond language (not to say ideology) as she proposes. In reviewing her suffering from that distance, Jane Rochester is replacing the child's subversive discourse of revolution with the more conservative and socialized discourse of domesticity.

We are isolating these discourses of revolution and domesticity in order to show what is ideologically at stake, not only in the text's conflicting representations of Jane's subjectivity, but also in its recuperation of a coherent and unified subject in Jane Rochester. Because of its heterogeneous encoding of cultural discourses, this text produces an excess of ideological effects, while its narrative structure attempts to manage this excess, primarily through the hermeneutic and symbolic codes. The discourse of revolution, which positions Jane as a subject of "discord," is one of the text's many sites of excessive meaning, and the narrative's closure tames this discourse, first by combining it with the discourse of domesticity, then by replacing it with that discourse so as to position Jane as the subject of "concord." Once this happens, rebellion is drained of its political meaning and domesticity is likewise protected from any real politics by its simple equation with concord.

Even at the pressure-point of closure, however, a text can never fully contain its excess of discursive activity. In *Jane Eyre* important issues of class and gender differences, and of national and religious ideologies, are merely regulated, not subsumed by, hermeneutic questions of domestic passion, moral rewards and punishments, and personal freedom. Most obviously, the discourse of puritanical religion (and not the discourse of domesticity) gets the last word with Jane's reading of a letter from St John Rivers, who is still searching for his heavenly reward. Quoting Revelation 22:20, he confides in Jane: "My Master . . . has forewarned me. Daily He announces more distinctly, 'Surely I come quickly!' and hourly I more eagerly respond, 'Amen; even so, come Lord Jesus!'" (398). The positioning of this discourse as the last paragraph of the text can be read doubly. On the one hand, it confirms closure by pointing up all the more the stability of the subject Jane Rochester in comparison to the inner torment of St John Rivers. On the other hand, it radically questions, if it does not entirely undermine, the "concord" of equality in Jane's marriage to Rochester by stressing service to yet another and higher Master. It thus threatens the discourse of domesticity which Jane cites to close her story. Further, if we were to retrace this discourse in the text, we would discover that it remains competitive with the discourses of revolution and domesticity, repeatedly inscribing additional sites of ideological contest.

Our purpose in analyzing *Jane Eyre* has been to illustrate the production of subjectivity out of the multiply encoded discourses of a text. The textual heterogeneity of *Jane Eyre* exceeds the ideological coherence of any single discourse, and thus writes the subject in contradiction. The narrative's closure, on the other hand, fixes the subject to a position of intelligibility or self-apprehension in a single discourse (in this case, that of domesticity) which appears to dominate, subsume, even transform others. Reinforcing the structuring of meaning through genre (discussed in chapter 3), the hermeneutic imperative of closure contains discursive excess; it sets limits to the potentially subversive effect of textual heterogeneity by disclosing a coherent subject in culturally recognizable terms. Decoding the text resists those limits because it exposes possibilities of alternative discursive alignments and, hence, allows for other possibilities of subjectivity. At stake in narrative, we are arguing, is the subject of narrative.

# 6
# The subject of narrative

Throughout the last two chapters we have been arguing that subjectivity is not a unified or transcendent psychological essence but a process. The subject, continually (re)activated and (re)positioned in the multiple discourses of culture, is an effect of signification. For the most part, however, we have concentrated on the textual representation of a divided and heterogeneous subject without taking the reader or viewer into account. As a result, we may have appeared to be implying the reader's or viewer's exemption from the discursive production of subjectivity. With this chapter, we shall explain that a narrative text does not simply represent subjectivity *to* readers or viewers; more importantly, it also signifies their subjectivity *for* them.

Previously we demonstrated that the speaking subject achieves a sense of self-presence as the originator of his or her utterance by identifying with the pronoun *I*. This signifier refers to its syntagmatic position in discourse for both its antecedent and its differential field of possible meanings; furthermore, it paradigmatically implies, and also locates in the discourse, the subject whom the utterance addresses, *you*. Drawing upon psychoanalysis and its elaboration of the linguistic model, this chapter will show that a narrative representation of subjectivity functions similarly as a signifier with which a reader or viewer identifies.

To illustrate how a text signifies the subjectivity of a reader by involving him or her in a process of identification, we return to Italo Calvino's *If on a winter's night a traveler*. Because this text addresses you explicitly as the subject of narration, it foregrounds, as conventional narrations do not, the extent to which your subjectivity as a reader depends upon identification with the signifier *you*.

Chapter 1 of *If on a winter's night a traveler* begins by narrating *you* as the subject of the event "reading" in a story sequence. "You are about to begin reading Italo Calvino's new novel, *If on a winter's night a traveller*" (Calvino 1981: 3). An effaced narrating agency makes itself apparent only indirectly in the form of imperatives and questions. "Relax. Concentrate. Dispel every other thought. Let the world around you fade" (3). You find a comfortable position, adjust the light, shut out distracting noise. "Anything else?" you are asked. "Do you have to pee? All right, you know best" (4).

You then begin reading a novel, which appears as a separate text entitled "If on a winter's night a traveler." This text starts a spy or crime story narrated by a character who reveals very little about himself, only that he is a messenger for "the organization." Arriving at a train station, he has been instructed to switch suitcases with an unknown contact for whom he now waits. At last, the police chief arrives at the station and, whispering that something has gone wrong, informs the narrator that he has only three minutes to get away or be arrested. Finding himself caught in some kind of mysterious game in which he is a powerless and ignorant player, the narrator, still carrying the suitcase, gets on another train . . .

That story stops. Chapter 2 again addresses you as the main character. You put down the book you have been reading because it is a defective copy, containing only that initial segment reprinted several times over. Wanting to know the outcome of the interrupted story, you return to the bookstore as soon as possible to exchange your book. Here you meet the Other Reader, Ludmilla, who is in the same predicament. The bookseller only adds to your frustration when he informs you of an additional printing error: the bindery has mixed up the Calvino novel with another new book, *Outside the town of*

*Malbork* by Tazio Bazakbal, and this latter novel is the one you have actually started.

After exchanging phone numbers with the Other Reader, you return home to continue reading the Bazakbal novel – but "from the very first page you realize that the novel you are holding has nothing to do with the one you were reading yesterday" (33). Even worse, once you become interested in this new story (which appears as a second titled segment, "Outside the town of Malbork"), you discover another printer's error: "at the moment when your attention is gripped by the suspense, in the middle of a decisive sentence, you turn the page and find yourself facing two blank sheets" (42).

These two unrelated and unfinished segments typify how the book you read short-circuits the completion of story again and again. Although "you want to go forward, without stopping" (76), ten different story segments each initiate a new hermeneutic code without ever leading to resolution; and these segments alternate with the twelve numbered chapters recounting your frustrated efforts to complete any of the stories you start reading (as a character) at actual points (chapter breaks) in the text. Because "for you the only thing that matters now is to continue your reading" (115), these repeated interruptions and postponements finally cause you to complain, "everything has been going wrong for me: it seems to me that in the world there now exists only stories that remain suspended or get lost along the way" (257).

Increasing your investment in narrative every time it begins a new story but deferring your satisfaction every time it fails to complete any story at all, *If on a winter's night a traveler* narrates *you* as a reader who, expecting "books to be read from beginning to end" (257), actively seeks narrative closure as a source of pleasure. You thus hope that "somewhere the complete volume must exist" (115), and it does, in the book you are reading. Not only have you in fact been reading it from beginning to end, but all along you have been functioning as the subject of events in a particular kind of narrative, a romance: boy meets girl, boy pursues girl, boy gets girl. The pleasure you sought in a story's completion, you discover, cannot, in fact, be separated from your desire for Ludmilla, the Other Reader whom you met in the bookshop in chapter 2. "The pursuit of the interrupted book, which instilled in you a special excitement since you were conducting it together with the Other Reader, turns out to be the same thing as pursuing her, who eludes you in a proliferation of mysteries, deceits, disguises" (151). This double quest arranges a metaphoric resemblance between reading and desiring. When "you are in bed together, you two Readers," her body as well as yours becomes "an object of reading" in the course of your lovemaking (154–5). Further, the novel closes with the fulfillment of your desire for both the completed book and the Other Reader. In the end you marry Ludmilla and, lying alongside your wife in "a great double bed [which] receives your parallel readings," you inform her, "I've almost finished *If on a winter's night a traveler* by Italo Calvino" (260).

From the first moment it addresses you as its reader, *If on a winter's night a traveler* narrates your subjectivity as the signified of reading.

> This book so far has been careful to leave open to the Reader who is reading the possibility of identifying himself with the Reader who is read: this is why he was not given a name, which would automatically have made him the equivalent of a Third Person, of a character (whereas to you, as Third Person, a name had to be given, Ludmilla), and so he has been kept a pronoun in the abstract condition of pronouns, suitable for any attribute and any action. (141)

Yet, despite the claim that *you* designates a universal Reader, this pronoun turns out to be a quite specific and concrete signifier because of its location in discourse. The text tells you what *you* do (your functions as the primary actor in the story) and who *you* are (your traits as the character who is also the story's reader). A sophisticate who has lost faith in pleasure, "you're the sort of person who, on principle, no longer expects anything of anything." As far as reading is concerned, you make it the one exception to your weary, cynical view because you do not take the pleasure it offers seriously: "you believe that you may still grant yourself legitimately this youthful pleasure of expectation in a carefully circumscribed area like the field of books, where you can be lucky or unlucky, but the risk of disappointment isn't serious" (4). Or so you think, since your impulsiveness, exasperation, and impatience at finding the printer's error in the first segment impel your quest to finish the story. The text thus demonstrates for you what you have forgotten: that a narrative places its reader in a field of desire which gives reading its sense of urgency.

This narrated subject desiring closure, furthermore, cannot be separated from the specific cultural discourses in which *you* find your subjectivity. For instance, as the passage quoted above reveals, the second-person address of the text has, as its antecedent, another pronoun, *he*; and this gender specificity invites the reader to identify with a masculine narrative, a "boy meets girl story," and the cultural meanings that this structure encodes. In chapter 3 we argued that a genre structures cultural representations of sexual difference. The story of *If on a winter's night a traveler* places a male *you* in relation to a female "other" – semically traited as mysterious, unattainable, and unreadable – thereby organizing its representation of *your* subjectivity around her as the object of your desire. Identifying with this masculine *you* has serious consequences. Through the signifier *you*, this narrative symbolically encodes gender difference by granting the male reader direct and the female reader indirect access to subjectivity. A male reader attains subjectivity as the text's narrated subject and recognizes his "masculinity" but only through a stand-in (the pronoun, the character), a signifier of having a lack (you are he but not the he who is *you*). A female reader can identify with the same narrated subject of the text and recognize her "femininity" but only by identifying with a signifier of being a lack (she is not the he who is *you*).

Either way, identification with the pronoun *you* has an effect of alienation. It dispels the illusion that "you have entered the novel" as a fully autonomous individual (69) and exposes instead what such imaginary habitation requires of you: occupying the position in discourse where the signifier *you* appears in place of you. Recognizing him- or herself in the signifier *you*, a reader gains the pleasure of being signified as a coherent subject, but loses, we want to emphasize, autonomy from the discourse in which that pronoun appears. In other words, you may exist independently of the text and its discursive representation of your subjectivity, but you cannot mean independently of it.

Psychoanalytic theory offers a powerful explanation of the relation between narrative and subjectivity that we have begun to raise through our discussion of *If on a winter's night a traveler*. Developed largely by Sigmund Freud from the 1890s to the 1930s in Vienna, *psychoanalysis* is both a treatment of mental illnesses and a theory of the unconscious representation of desire.[1] Psychoanalysis has been popularized and oversimplified as a psychology of a universal human nature; it is therefore all too easy to minimize the radical implications which psychoanalysis poses, in its theory and in its practice, for an understanding of the relations among language, culture, and subjectivity. Challenging the assumption that subjectivity is a state of self-presence, psychoanalysis asserts that every subject is split, divided between conscious and unconscious, and that this splitting occurs as a result of the subject's entrance into the symbolic field of culture through the acquisition of language.

According to Freud, psychoanalysis "defines what is mental as processes such as feeling, thinking and willing, and it is obliged to maintain that there is *unconscious* thinking and *unapprehended* willing" (Freud 1977: 22; our italics). The unconscious designates "a particular realm of the mind with its own wishful impulses, its own mode of expression and its peculiar mental mechanisms which are not in force elsewhere" (Freud 1977: 212). In his various writings Freud explained the unconscious in biological terms as the seat of instincts, in physical terms as an economical discharge of energy, and most familiarly in psychical terms as that which is not immediately available to memory or that which is repressed. While he claimed, "our therapy works by transforming what is unconscious into what is conscious," he also acknowledged that the unconscious may be "*permanently* unconscious and not merely 'latent at the time'" (Freud 1977: 280, 148). He repeatedly emphasized that the unconscious should not be misunderstood as an originary, natural state of instinct to which we could return if only the bar of repression were lifted. On the contrary, the repression of instinct, demanded by the child's acculturation, produces the unconscious and inaugurates desiring subjectivity. The formation of the unconscious through repression divides a bodily need from its means of gratification, a drive which does not (cannot) fulfill the need but represents its gratification as a fantasized potentiality: desire, "the picturing of its own fulfillment" (Freud 1977: 372).

An example chosen by Freud in *Beyond the Pleasure Principle* (1920), and also noted in the earlier *Interpretation of Dreams* (1900), clearly illustrates this division. At the age of a year and a half, Freud's grandson would habitually throw away or hide his toys, saying "o–o–o–o" as he did so. Interpreting this sound as the child's articulation of the German word *fort* or "gone," Freud argued that this puzzling behavior amounted to a game: the child was playing at making the toys "gone."

> One day I made an observation which confirmed my view. The child had a wooden reel with a piece of string tied round it. It never occurred to him to pull it along on the floor behind him, for instance, and play at its being a carriage. What he did was to hold the reel by the string and very skilfully throw it over the end of his curtained cot, so that it disappeared into it, at the same time uttering his expressive "o–o–o–o." He then pulled the reel out of the cot again by the string and hailed its reappearance with a joyful "*da*" ["there"]. This, then, was the complete game – disappearance and return. As a rule one only witnessed its first act, which was repeated untiringly as a game in itself, though there is no doubt that the greater pleasure was attached to the second act. (Freud 1961: 9)

Freud introduced this example to describe how a child succeeds in gaining control over the painful lived experience of separation from his mother through a representation of absence, the game, which compensates by replacing the actual event and feelings. The *fort/da* game

> was related to the child's great cultural achievement – the instinctual renunciation (that is, the renunciation of instinctual satisfaction) which he had made in allowing his mother to go away without protesting. He compensated himself for this, as it were, by himself staging the disappearance and return of the objects within his reach. (Freud 1961: 9)

As the repeated game increasingly distances the child from the referential experience of his mother's absence and presence, it also directs his desire towards a representation that yields greater pleasure through repetition.

Unconscious desire is, quite literally, *not* conscious; it is made visible only through some form of representation – a slip of the tongue, a joke, a dream, a symptom, a game, a text. Psychoanalytic treatment concentrates on the ways in which language manifests these traces of the unconscious in the patient's speech. This close attention to language shows that speech does not unify subjectivity by transforming unconsciousness into consciousness but, on the contrary, continually manifests the division of a subject. The contemporary psychoanalyst Jacques Lacan describes the division of subjectivity in terms of the gap opened up between speaking subject and subject of speech. "It is not a question of knowing whether I speak of myself in a way that conforms to what I am," he comments, "but rather of knowing whether I am the same as that of which I speak" (Lacan 1977: 165). The subject gains meaning in language ("I speak"), but only at the expense of being ("I am").

> Let us illustrate this with what we are dealing with here, namely, the being of the subject, that which is there beneath the meaning. If we choose being, the subject disappears, it eludes us, it falls into non-meaning. If we choose meaning, the meaning survives only deprived of that part of non-meaning that is, strictly speaking, that which constitutes in the realization of the subject, the unconscious. (Lacan 1978: 211)

Subjectivity occurs through this signifying exchange of meaning for being: the signifier "represents the subject for another signifier, which other signifier has as its effect the *aphanisis* [fading] of the subject" (Lacan 1978: 218). The speaking subject appears in discourse as a subject of speech, but only as a condition of lacking, in the sense of not being present except at "a second degree of otherness," that is, in the space of the unconscious and its "discourse of the Other" (Lacan 1977: 172).

Basing his claims on a reading of Freud, Lacan attributes the continuous and permanent division of the subject to the effect of language. "What the psychoanalytic experience discovers in the unconscious is the whole structure of language," and this discovery, Lacan demonstrates, requires a rethinking of the unconscious either as something recoverable in consciousness or as purely biological instincts (Lacan 1977: 147). The unconscious produces meaning through the same support that characterizes the signifying chains of language: the syntagmatic axis of addition and combination and the paradigmatic axis of selection and substitution. A symptom, such as an obsessive act or worry, paradigmatically substitutes for another signifier (an unconscious desire), which then appears as an unconscious signified of this metaphoric equation. The symptom, in other words, represses the subject's position between two signifiers (i.e. the signifier represents a subject for another signifier), where a relation of metonymy causes a sliding, not a fixing, of signification along the chain of unconscious as well as conscious discourse. There is, as a consequence, no fixed binding of signifier to signified in the mental life of a subject but, rather, a frenetic slippage of signification resembling the play of textuality.

To explain this sliding, we need to consider how and why the subject's relation to a signifier is, in the Lacanian scheme, both imaginary and symbolic. The *imaginary* is that register of subjectivity achieved through identification with a phantom or an image, as in a mirror. For example, in the *fort/da* game, Lacan comments, the child attains control over the event by identifying with the reel as an imaginary signifier of his subjectivity.

> This reel is not the mother reduced to a little ball . . . it is a small part of the subject that detaches itself from him while still remaining his, still retained. . . . If it is true that the signifier is the first mark of the subject, how can we fail to recognize here – from the very fact that this game is accompanied by one of the first oppositions to appear – that it is in the object to which the opposition is applied in act, the reel, that we must designate the subject. (Lacan 1978: 62)

The sound "o–o–o–o" accompanying the tossing of the reel also serves as an imaginary signifier of the child's subjectivity, which becomes clear in Freud's observation that "as a rule" the child repeatedly played only the first moment – "gone" – as a game in and of itself. Freud's footnote to this example, in fact, shows the extent to which the child's subjectivity becomes further linked to an imaginary representation (signifier) of his own disappearance.

> One day the child's mother had been away for several hours and on her return was met with the words "Baby o–o–o–o!" which was at first incomprehensible. It soon turned out, however, that during this long period of solitude the child had found a method of making *himself* disappear. He had discovered his reflection in a full-length mirror which did not quite reach to the ground, so that by crouching down he could make his mirror-image "gone." (Freud 1961: 9)

Premised on a division of the "I" from an "Other" (a "not-I"), the imaginary register of the *fort/da* game marks the child's ability to identify with a signifier of his own subjectivity and, through this identification, to gain pleasure, the content-ment that results from being and having content. However, since the imaginary only awards a fictive sense of being full and unified, identification amounts to self-alienation, as being fades into imaginary meaning.

Reading Freud's description of the *fort/da* game, Lacan observes two different moments of signification taking place for the child. The child's identification with the signifier – "o–o–o–o," the reel, his own body – places him in the imaginary register, which is why he takes pleasure simply in playing "gone." But, as Lacan goes on to show, the pairing of *fort* with *da* involves an exchange of signs that places the child in the signifying chain of language too. The child represents his needs in terms of something they are not: *two* signifiers structured as a binary, "which is a *here or there*, and whose aim, in its alternation, is simply that of being the *fort* of a *da* and the *da* of a *fort*" (Lacan 1978: 63). The play of difference in this opposition excludes the absent mother and the strong feelings of love and hostility (the drives) connected to her disappearance. As a result, when playing the complete game of *fort/da*, the child's use of the binary pair exemplifies his entrance into the symbolic field of culture as inaugurated by his full acquisition of language.[2]

Whereas imaginary plenitude occurs through the unifying relation of a duality – the subject and the missing complement – the *symbolic* register of language and culture introduces a mediating third term to structure subjectivity around a lack, thereby providing the subject access, not to pleasure, but to desire. Desire opposes pleasure. It is dis-contenting, unstructured excess, "the 'remainder' of the subject, something which is always left over, but which has no content as such" (Rose 1986: 55), or, as Lacan calls it, "the non-representative representative" (Lacan 1978: 218). For the subject to desire someone or something, desire must first have been organized around a division of the object from the subject.[3] A subject can desire only in terms of the division that occurs through a symbolic representation of the desired object. Lacan names that which "serves as a symbol of the lack" the *objet a* (Lacan 1978: 103). This privileged signifier substitutes or stands in for the subject's desire but is not identical to it; rather, it symbolizes the impossibility of ever satisfying desire completely. The *fort/da* game organizes the child's subjectivity around a signifier of lack (the reel as the *objet a*), which, in turn, represents his desire for mother as a signifier of his own lacking.[4]

Lacan calls the symbolic structuring of desiring subjectivity a self-mutilation, a metaphorically castrating act. Unlike the imaginary, which awards a sense of plenitude, the symbolic awards a sense of emptiness: hence the wounding connotation of castration. As in Freud's account, the importance of symbolic castration becomes crucial in understanding the cultural regulation of desire. Castration structures unconscious desire through the *objet a* to signify a lacking and desiring subject.

The symbolic register provides the terms by which culture engenders subjectivity through its organization of unconscious desires. As Lacan describes them, these terms are quite specific to the patriarchal order of modern western culture. During the Oedipal crisis, which is the inauguration of full entry into the symbolic register, the Father triangulates the dual relationship of Mother and Child. Representing the Law of the Father as the prohibition of the Child's desire for the Mother, the *phallus* (not to be confused with the anatomical organ, a penis) then symbolically regulates desire through the threat of castration. The symbolic register constructs desiring subjectivity along an axis of gender based on the subject's relation to the phallus "in so far as it is lacking" (Lacan 1978: 103), that is, as the *objet a* privileged by western culture. Male and female are differentiated in terms of the opposition having/lacking the phallus. In relation to the castrating lack symbolized by the phallus, the male subject says: I have that lack, and the female subject says: I am that lack.[5]

We are speaking here of male and female not as biological entities so much as symbolic positions with which a subject identifies. "Sexuality only exists through its social forms and social organization," and "the unconscious – with its own dynamic, rules, and history, [is] where the biological possibilities of the body acquire meaning" (Weeks 1986: 24, 61). As we illustrated in our discussion of the symbolic code in chapter 5, the symbolic register establishes the slash of sexual difference – the phallus is that (castrating, dividing, wounding) symbol of difference. A culturally defined "male" identifies with the signifier of having the phallus (being fullness), while a culturally defined "female" identifies with the signifier of lacking the phallus (being lack). The two different relations to the phallus stabilize sexual identity for culture, regulating desire so as to forbid the transgressions symbolized by the castrato and the androgyne (homosexuality, bisexuality, transvestism, transsexuality, asexuality). "The phallus," Jacqueline Rose explains, "stands for the moment when prohibition must function . . . it signals to the subject that 'having' only functions as the price of a loss and 'being' as an effect of division" (Rose 1986: 64). If, in this western patriarchal mythology of sexual difference, the male must *have* the phallus as the cultural price of attaining his gender, he can only lose the plenitude he desires. And his conformity, regulated through the threat of negated desire symbolized by the castrato, ensures the suppression of gender transgression: male homosexuality. Similarly, if the female must *be* the phallus as the cultural price of attaining her gender, she can only be doubly divided from plenitude, split as the object of male desire and the subject of her own; in Mary Ann Doane's words, the female can only "desire to desire . . . striving for an access to a desiring subjectivity" (Doane 1987: 122). The female's conformity, regulated through the threat of excessive desire symbolized by the androgyne, likewise ensures the suppression of gender transgression: lesbianism. The phallus is thus the culturally privileged symbol around which value accrues to organize, engender, and license culturally orthodox desire *in the unconscious*.

The symbolic organization of gendered identities tends to appear natural because it coincides with biological difference. However, the unconscious trace of not being symbolically engendered disrupts the fixed binary of he/she. Shifts can occur simultaneously within the subject's apparently fixed gendered identity. A male can take up a female position while remaining biologically male, and a female can take up a male position while remaining biologically female. Desire moves on from signifier to signifier (like textuality), never finally resting on one object (one signified). Just as a final meaning cannot be determined, final satisfaction of desire is out of reach. Indeed, desire admits of no full satisfaction or it is not desire. Consequently, in its organization of desire, the symbolic cannot ensure the stability of gender or banish transgression entirely; this excess appears in the unconscious, not merely as a remainder, but as a reminder of what cannot be symbolically contained. Because of this excess we can articulate a role for the unconscious in opposition to the regulatory functions of the symbolic. Excess can be viewed not only as that which is left over but as resistance, the surfeit which always threatens to disrupt.

To many, the psychoanalytic narrative of development, typified in our account by the *fort/da* example, implies a subject moving from the imaginary to the symbolic and becoming fixed there. The Lacanian reading of Freud, however, stresses the subject's continual oscillation between these two registers in adult life as well as in childhood.

> Language in the realm of the imaginary is understood in terms of some full relation between word and thing; a mysterious unity of sign and referent. In the symbolic, language is understood in terms of lack and absence – the sign finds its definition diacritically through the absent syntagmatic and paradigmatic chains it enters into. As speaking subjects we constantly oscillate between the symbolic and the imaginary – constantly imagining ourselves granting some full meaning to the words we speak, and constantly being surprised to find them determined by relations outside our control. (MacCabe 1985: 65)

Divided between lack and excess, the symbolically produced subject must repeatedly be reconstituted as a coherent "I" in discourse. Discourse offers the subject a position from which to articulate or grasp meaning; this position, however, is in fact occupied, not by the subject, but by a signifier. The production of subjectivity therefore necessitates the *suturing* of the subject to discourse through the signifier.

Lacan mentions *suture* only in passing as "the conjunction of the imaginary and the symbolic" (Lacan 1978: 118). Jacques-Alain Miller has expanded upon Lacan's remark to argue that "suture names the relation of the subject to the chain of its discourse . . . [where] it figures as the element which is lacking, in the form of a stand-in" (J.-A. Miller 1977–8: 25–6).

Subjectivity is achieved in discourse *through* suture and *as* a suture. Like the surgical closing of a wound, the suturing of the divided subject involves both the operation, the binding of subject to signifier, and what the operation produces, the binding that leaves a trace of their division. This is why suture results in a conjunction of the imaginary and symbolic registers. Suture induces pleasure through the subject's imaginary identification with a signifier, which compensates for the symbolic lack (castration) that structures desire; but unstructured desire repeatedly tears the suture, thereby necessitating additional suturing along the chain of discourse, where the subject only achieves "the possibility of one signifier more" (J.-A. Miller 1977–8: 33). The replacement of the subject by a "stand-in" amounts to a series of displacements along the discursive chain, with each moment of lack marking a "cut" that requires suturing. Subjectivity is, consequently, never fixed but continuous, and therein lies the possibility of intervention in the symbolic and the need to examine the suturing of the subject in cultural structures like narrative.

Our particular interest in psychoanalysis arises from its usefulness for theorizing the relation of readers and viewers to narrative in terms of pleasure while still accounting for the heterogeneity and division of desiring subjectivity. Reading or viewing narrative, we are arguing, involves the continuous suturing of a narrated subject whose pleasure is secured, jeopardized, and resecured by a signifier.

Discussions of narrative and suture have concentrated on

film rather than prose because the technological apparatus of film calls attention to a process of suture at the site of the text's production. The production of a film takes place without regard for narrative continuity. Scenes are photographed out of order and the final version of a single scene often includes shots collected from numerous takes. Likewise, the sound track (which includes music and effects as well as dialogue) is not always recorded or even edited at the same time as the visual track; rather, the two are spliced together in the last stages of post-production. A cinematic text thus materially consists of celluloid frames which are themselves sutured, although most commercial films efface signs of their segmentation through the diegetic codes of cinematic narration. These link a close-up of a face or hand, say, to a shot of the entire body in another frame, just as they perpetuate the illusion of presence when a stand-in doubles for an actor physically or vocally, or when one scene has been shot partly on location and partly on a studio set.

The compilation of a whole film out of pieces further under-scores the need for additional suturing during its exhibition. In a theater, the viewer must imagine continuity out of what is actually textual discontinuity, reels of edited celluloid frames projected by a machine onto a screen. Along the syntagmatic chain of images that comprise the edited film "separate frames have between them differences that are indispensable for the creation of an illusion of continuity, of a continuous passage (movement, time). But only on one condition can these differ-ences create this illusion: they must be effaced as differences" (Baudry 1986: 290). A film appears to move in time because its footage consists of frames that visually differ from each other. In and of itself, each frame of a film is a textual cut or segment sutured together in the narration in order to establish the viewing subject as "the *point* of the film's spatial relations" (Heath 1981: 54). By providing an apparently stable position which fixes the signifying activity of the text, the film sutures the viewer to discourse through the signifier.

The typical commercial film lures the viewer into collaborat-ing with this process of suture by effacing signs of a narrating subject; it treats the camera as "the (invisible) seeing agency of the film itself as discourse, as the agency which *puts forward* the story and shows it to us" (Metz 1982: 96). So, for example, whenever a mirror reflects the opposing space of a shot – the space presumably occupied by the narrating subject in relation to the focalized image – no signs of the camera photographing the mirror appear on the screen (see figure 10). The screen, however, clearly divides the narrating subject, located at the site of the film's production, from the narrated subject, located at the site of its exhibition. The camera (and its stand-in in the auditorium, the projector) exposes the viewer's absence from the site of the narrative, the screen. To compensate for being absent from that narrative space, the viewer seeks to identify with the camera but only finds a signifier, the subject of narration standing in for the narrating subject.

Figure 10, from the film *Lady in the Lake* (1946; dir. Robert Montgomery), exemplifies this theoretical argument. Simulating the effect of first-person prose narration, the film's diegesis focalizes exclusively through one character, Philip Marlow, played by Robert Montgomery, with the camera appearing in his place, showing only what he sees. Philip Marlow's absence from the screen encourages the viewer to identify with the

*Figure 10*

camera and its gaze, its spatial point of view, as the source of the cinematic enunciation (the imagery). Every time another character addresses Marlow – speaks to him, kisses him, hits him – that character looks at or approaches the camera and appears to address the viewer. As a result, the viewer seems to occupy the same position in relation to the narrative that Marlow does, which is the position of the effaced camera as the agency putting the story forward. The only visual indication of Marlow's presence in the diegesis occurs whenever the camera looks at a reflecting surface, as it does in figure 10, and the actor appears in the camera's place. Robert Montgomery should be in the frame, standing behind Audrey Totter (the other performer), but he is not. Filling up that empty space with his image, the mirror reflects the signifier (Marlow) as a stand-in for the absent viewer.

Figure 10 is a still, a static image from a *moving* picture: a series of shots, each motivating the viewer's relation to a signifier by encouraging – only to jeopardize – identification with the camera. To illustrate, the key discussions of suture (see Oudart 1977–8; Dayan 1976; Heath 1981; Silverman 1983) all cite the convention of shot/reverse-shot editing. In this diegetic encoding of focalization, one shot shows a field of vision and the second establishes the perspective of the first by exposing its reverse, the other side. *The Letter*, for example, displays the metaphoric comparison of Leslie Crosbie's passion and the moonlit sky, previously discussed in chapter 2, through shot/reverse-shot editing: first a close-up of Leslie (Bette Davis) looking, followed by a cut to the moonlit sky, then another close-up of Leslie. With the reverse shot identifying the object of Leslie's gaze (the sky), the diegesis attributes this second perspective to a subject of narration, the character inhabiting the narrated space of the first shot and looking at an absent reverse field. The character's perspective in the diegesis therefore determines the oppositional relation between one field of vision and its other side. At the same time, the camera also focalizes upon Leslie; it shows the viewer what she looks at and also shows her looking from an angle which she herself cannot possibly visualize. Together, these shots establish a totalizing position for the viewer that appears to be identical to the narrating subject's.

While not absolutely necessary for the suturing effect of cinematic narration, shot/reverse-shot editing exemplifies how the cutting of a film subjects the viewer to a process of suture as the only means of identifying with the camera's position of visual coherence and plenitude.

> The cut guarantees that both the preceding and the subsequent shots will function as structuring absences to the present shot. These absences make possible a signifying ensemble, convert one shot into a signifier of the next one, and the signified of the preceding one. (Silverman 1983: 205)

In the example from *The Letter*, the metaphoric resemblance of Leslie and the moonlit sky, syntagmatically arranged by the two shots, fixes signifier to signified and thereby puts forward a full and closed sign. The actual cutting of the film, however, insists upon the value of both shots as two adjacent signifiers: hence the return to the first shot after the reverse.

When taken separately, each shot exposes the viewing subject as lacking, excluded from the diegesis. The spectacle on screen of an actor looking implies a direction for that gaze which should include the viewer as the subject of visual address; but, when the reverse shot displays the focalized point of that gaze, a stand-in appears in the viewer's place. This threat of absence motivates the viewer's identification with the signifying chain of the text, where, as in the *fort/da* game, the imaginary plenitude of the camera's all-encompassing look makes good the viewer's symbolic lack, and a castrating exchange of meaning for being occurs. For while identification sutures the viewer to the signifier and leads to his or her investment in the text as a source of pleasure, the editing of the film repeatedly tears each prior moment of suture, exposing the cut that signifies the viewer's lack and necessitating, not only a continuation of the suturing process, but also an investment in the symbolic field of the signifier.

Identifying with the signifier, a viewer is sutured to the discourse where that signifier appears; the suturing process, which constitutes the viewer as a narrated subject, the imaginary producer of symbolic meaning, thus helps to account for the powerful interpellating effects of a film. The example we have been using from *The Letter* intertextually cites, through the familiar metaphoric equation of feminine desire and the moon, a discourse of gender that interpellates the viewer to an ortho- dox ideological representation of the female as an enigmatic set of contradictions. In one shot Leslie's look signifies her mystery and passion, while in the other shot the object of her look signifies her repression and purity. This discourse supplies, in the form of the metaphor, a signified for the pair of shots: Leslie's desire is the enigma of womanhood, the knowledge which the male desires but can never attain. Sutured to this discourse, the viewer takes up an orthodox position of gender in the symbolic order of patriarchal culture. A masculine narrated subject identifies with *having* a signifier of female desire (the enigma) as the object of his own desire, while a feminine narrated subject identifies with *being* that signifier which the male desires.

Neither subject position is necessarily aligned to the viewer's biological gender; for that matter, the editing of the initial sequences endorses, for male and female viewers alike, a mascu- line subject position with respect to Leslie's enigmatic look. After opening with her shooting of Hammond, the narration cuts away from her looking down at the body, shows the workers' bungalow, where one of the men, awakened by the gunfire, looks up at the moon in a shot/reverse-shot sequence, and cuts back to Leslie who, in two shot/reverse-shot forma- tions, first looks down at the body and then, duplicating the gaze of the male worker, looks up at the moon. In the first shot/ reverse-shot segment, the moon attracts the male gaze when it goes behind the clouds, while in the second one the light of the reemerging moon draws Leslie's gaze away from Hammond's body. Leslie thus occupies a position which the narration first attributes to a masculine viewer in the diegesis and then paradigmatically engenders as the inverse of the masculine: that is, in response to the shooting, the male viewing subject sees the enigma of the feminine look and the shadow she casts.

Far from continuously suturing the viewer to the symbolic order, though, a film can actually intensify the suturing process by putting in jeopardy and then resecuring orthodox symbolic positions. In *The Letter*, such a transgressive moment occurs when Leslie goes to retrieve the incriminating letter from Mrs Hammond. With Mrs Hammond's entrance, shot/reverse-shot cutting at first emphasizes the racial difference of the two women through the same coding of western/oriental that differentiates Leslie and her lawyer, Howard Joyce, from Ong Chi Seng, his assistant, and Chung Hi, the go-between. Leslie is pale, English-speaking, covered by a white lace shawl, whereas Mrs Hammond is dark, speaks Malay and Chinese, and is bejeweled. At the same time, a display of sexual difference coopts the spectacle of racial difference. The shot of Leslie along with the three men looking at Mrs Hammond, shown in the reverse shot, makes Leslie's viewing position inseparable from the racial and gendered discourses which together constitute the other woman as a symbolic Other, the opposite of the white civilized Englishwoman. Mrs Hammond, in short, is the phallic signifier: she has control over the letter, the metonymy of Leslie's illicit feminine desire, which Leslie must repudiate in order to remain within the symbolic order of her own culture and its Law.

The next shot/reverse-shot segments, however, expose a rift in this orthodox symbolic ordering of difference. As Leslie approaches Mrs Hammond, the editing noticeably emphasizes each woman's stare, so that identification through looking becomes more important than the letter as a signifier of feminine desire. The camera excludes the men from the frame at this point to focalize on and through the two women, who, in a series of shot/reverse-shot segments, alternate as signifiers and signifieds of each other's gaze. Displaying the two women as mirror images, this sequence of editing discourages the viewer from identifying with either woman's look alone, leading to a moment of suturing that allows for imaginary resistance to the symbolic order endorsed elsewhere in the film. In the reciprocity of this looking, the spectacle of imaginary rapport with a signifier disturbs its position in the symbolic chain of antithesis, where the female is the negation of the male and, hence, the object of his desire. The repetition of the viewer in the viewed removes the cut or slash that makes one the other's reverse, and this unstructuring of desire reveals the precarious position of the desiring subject in the symbolic.

That potentially transgressive moment of suture does not pose a serious threat to the film's endorsement of the orthodox symbolic order of gender and race for several reasons. The text encodes racial difference even in these shots, and it restores the patriarchal discourse of gender immediately afterwards, thereby narrating a viewing subject whose investment in the symbolic is actually increased by its momentary disruption. Moreover, a viewer of *The Letter* can even override this potentially transgressive point in the narration by suturing through the film's story. Just as cinematic narration paradigmatically increases the value of each successive shot as the deferred or absent signified of the textual syntagm, so a film's story also encourages the viewer to identify with events as signifiers of lack appearing in a signifying chain. One event (such as Leslie's meeting with Mrs Hammond) functions as a signifier of what happens next, the succeeding event (the trial, where the suppression of the letter leads to Leslie's acquittal), and so on, until the story's closure reveals the final signified (Mrs Hammond's murder of Leslie) that arrests further movement along this chain. In its parallelism to the opening, the closing event of *The Letter* replaces one form of justice (the British legal system) by another (the retribution enacted by Mrs Hammond); and, while this alternative law is encoded as native and feminine, it still punishes Leslie for her crime, her dishonesty, and her desire. Like most mainstream films, this one "duplicates within the fiction as a whole the paradigm of the shot/reverse shot, disrupting the existing symbolic order, dislocating the subject-positions within it, and challenging its ideals of coherence and fullness only in order subsequently to re-affirm that order, those positions, and those ideals" (Silverman 1983: 221). Containing Leslie's transgression in its closure, *The Letter* leaves intact the enigma of her feminine desire. By continually fracturing and resetting the signifying chain of the narrative, the structuring of the film's story can thus lead the viewer safely past a disrupting moment of suture in the narration, sustaining an investment in the symbolic even when the imaginary puts it in jeopardy.

In a film's story as well as in its narration, then, every point in the signifying chain, be it a shot or an event, functions as the signifier of the next, suturing the viewer to the chain as the possibility of one signifier more: the next shot, the next event. The process of suture is *anticipatory* at the level of the signifier and *retroactive* at the level of the signified (Oudart 1977–8: 37).

At the same time as the viewer sutures the film, by imagining continuity out of the text's discontinuity, the film, regulating its disruptive textual movement through its encoding of narrative structures, sutures the viewer as its narrated subject.

In showing how story sutures the viewer, we have already begun to indicate that the theory of suture can be extended to prose narrative without much difficulty. We have, in fact, already laid the ground for such analysis with our discussion of *If on a winter's night a traveler* at the start of this chapter.

*If on a winter's night a traveler* displays rather openly how prose narrative involves the reader in a process of suturing along lines similar to what we have been arguing about film. Like the cinematic image, the second-person address prevents the reader from identifying with the narrating subject, the agency responsible for the text's enunciation at the site of production: writing. Instead, the pronoun *you* encourages a strong imaginary identification with the subject of both narration and events, offering a mirror image of what occurs at the site of the text's consumption: reading. At the same time, however, the narration also threatens this imaginary attachment to the signifier whenever it exposes the reader's self-alienation or fading as a narrated subject oscillating between the imaginary and symbolic registers of language.

We can illustrate with an exemplary moment of suturing from the text. In concluding our discussion of the novel, we pointed out that the location of *you* in discourse supplies the pronoun with a gendered antecedent, the *he* which signifies "loss of the you, a catastrophe as terrible as the loss of the I" (Calvino 1981: 147). The narration calls explicit attention to this loss at one point when it addresses Ludmilla, the Other Reader, as *you* in place of the "male Second Person" (141). Don't worry, you are reassured, "the you that was shifted to the Other Reader can, at any sentence, be addressed to you again. You are always a possible you" (147). But the ease with which the narration can suddenly shift the antecedents of *you* suggests otherwise. The narrated subject is not a possible *you* so much as a possible *he*. No less than *I*, *you* poses an imaginary rapport between subject and signifier which the third-person pronoun interrupts. That pronoun locates the narrated reading subject in the symbolic order, where *he* and *she* differentiate between the possible meanings of either *you* or *I*. This disruption of imaginary identification by the symbolic marks the "castrating" cut which the reader traces over in identifying with the masculine narrated subject and which, as a result of the suture, leaves in the reader traces of the linguistic and, hence, cultural organization of subjectivity.

The issue of suture in prose, furthermore, does not apply only to an unconventional second-person narration which makes the reader's subjectivity an explicit issue. A very traditional novel like *Jane Eyre* also narrates the reader as a subject through the process of suture. Our analysis of *Jane Eyre* in chapter 4 showed how focalization divides the narrating subject (Jane Rochester) from the subject of narration (Jane Eyre), putting the latter forward as a signifier which comes between the reader and the agency of enunciation. The section from the novel which we analyzed illustrates this division in close detail. Each shift in focalization (the older Jane commenting on the younger Jane's quoted monologue, say, the child Jane looking at Brocklehurst and then being addressed by him) marks a cut in the narration requiring the reader to identify with the signifier as the only means of compensating for – suturing over – the lack which the disjunction exposes. Positioned along a chain of signifiers through such suturing, the reader of *Jane Eyre* gains pleasure through identification, the content-ment of meaning, because he or she assents to being narrated as a desiring subject with an investment in the symbolic order that is regulated by the narration. The novel's story likewise jeopardizes, resecures, and jeopardizes this investment, disjoining only to rejoin the reader's imaginary and symbolic relations to the signifier, and finally arresting all this movement in its closure, which fixes the reader along with Jane as a gendered and classed subject of the discourse of domesticity. As we explained in chapter 5, however, the radically shifting discursive ground of Jane's subjectivity throughout her narration calls the closing endorsement of this final subject position into question. Suturing the narrative thus implicates the reader in the struggle over cultural meanings which traverses the text through the multiple and incompatible discourses it encodes.

Accounting for a reader's or viewer's unconscious investment in narrative, the theory of suture explains why reading a novel or watching a film offers pleasure. Narrative unfolds as a chain of signifiers which, exceeding and delaying a final signified, excites and maintains the suturing process throughout the course of reading or viewing. Each "cut" of the text encourages identification with a signifier positioned along the chain, leaving behind tracings of desire (unpleasure) which disrupt the reader/viewer's secure relation to the symbolic order of culture by jeopardizing his or her imaginary history as a stable, continuous, and coherent subject. In response to this dis-ease, the reader/viewer sutures the text's segmentations, achieving coherence (content) by identifying with the signifier, and attaining pleasure (contentment) as a sutured narrated subject seeking reinsertion in the symbolic order of culture. The suturing process actually increases pleasure when it allows the reader/viewer to repeat the history of previous and orthodox suturings, not only those from earlier points in the text but those from other texts as well.

The theory of suture, in short, raises an important question about the cultural basis of narrative pleasure. For if there can be no reading or viewing without some form of suture, and no suture which is not, ultimately, ideological in its reinstatement of the orthodox symbolic order, how can one transform or even resist the regulation of pleasure which occurs through the suturing process?

To answer this question, suture must be understood as more than an unconscious process or a personal signifying exchange of being for meaning that occurs between individual readers/ viewers and particular texts. Rather, suture must also be considered in the light of what we have argued in chapter 5 about the multiple cultural codes traversing a text. As the codes which supply the basis of story and narration are repeated from one text to another, they regulate the suturing process so that it follows predictable patterns. The particular suturing effects of shot/reverse-shot editing in *The Letter*, for instance, depend upon a viewer's recognizing, in these segments, the semic and symbolic encoding of femininity as well as the diegetic reference code of point of view. Likewise, a viewer suturing to the anticipatory and retrospective signifying chain of the film's story can do so only by recognizing the proairetic encoding of sequentiality and by filtering that code through the hermeneutic code's imposition of a discernible and closed structure. In both cases, the coherence held out as the lure to suture is made possible through the film's encoding of cultural discourses, such as those of gender and race, which appear truthful simply because of their intertextual familiarity. Locating the suturing process in culture and its practices of signification, codes draw upon a competence in reading/viewing narrative that is historical. Not only codings of words and images but also the discourses in which they appear change over time. Since World War II the west's political, economic, and social position with respect to the east has historically altered the discourse of orientalism referentially encoded in *The Letter*'s representation of Singapore, so this discourse now situates the 1980s western viewer in relation to the east differently than it did in 1940.

Certain cultural codes retain their force in directing the suturing process, because narratives are produced and consumed at institutional sites. Discussions of suture in film foreground mediation by the cinematic apparatus, the technology of production and exhibition resulting from "the interactions of the economic and ideological conditions of existence of cinema at any moment in history" (Kuhn 1982: 197).[6] As an institution with an economic interest in maintaining the social structures of power, the cinematic apparatus regulates the consumption as well as the production of films, because it has an investment in narrating the viewer as a subject of the ideology which supports those structures. Mainstream films like *The Letter* train the viewer to suture in consistent and orthodox ways: attending to the codes which form the basis of a closed story and coherent point of view, and privileging the cultural references to familiar discourses, such as those of patriarchy and orientalism, which smooth over textual disruptions and ideological contradictions.

One can make the same claim about publishing and academic apparatuses. For example, the publication of many nineteenth-century novels serially and/or in three volumes, as well as their distribution through subscription libraries, supported a hermeneutic structure, like that of *Bleak House* and *Jane Eyre*, which regulates ideological coherence by challenging and then, in its closure, reinstating the orthodoxy of culturally dominant discourses. No less than a viewer, a 1980s reader cannot pretend to duplicate the reception of a novel at the time of its publication. Since its publication in 1847, *Jane Eyre* has been evaluated and reevaluated, interpreted and reinterpreted, imitated, parodied, adapted for film, television, and comic books. All of these "readings" of the novel invariably come between the text and a contemporary reader. More to the point, whereas this novel was originally received as a popular fiction, today it is studied in the university as a classic. The traditional academic apparatus of the classroom trains readers in a practice of reading which we described in chapter 2 as "literary competence." Reading *Jane Eyre* as literature attends to its universal significance, metaphoric coherence, and thematic unity, thereby silencing the threatening contradictions and heterogeneity that we isolated in our segmentations of the text.

The literature classroom privileges a certain reading practice and a select group of texts which comprise its canon, and with this book we aim to intervene in both. To be sure, our choice of examples has not strayed too far from the texts valued as literature. For illustration, this book has relied heavily on the Anglo-American canon (*Bleak House, Pride and Prejudice*, and *Jane Eyre*); but it has included as well popular narratives (*The Letter, Cathy*, the Woolrich ad) and contemporary Latin American and European novels (*Heartbreak Tango, If on a winter's night a traveler*). We might have gone even further in choosing narratives from before 1800 or experimental films and novels that, representing the subject in unorthodox ways, direct the suturing of a reader/viewer differently. However, we have wanted our examples to remain consistent with the kinds of narratives encountered every day in our culture, in the media as well as in the classroom. We have therefore chosen on purpose not to analyze representations of feminist, gay and lesbian, black, or Asian subjectivities. This task, we believe, can occur only after denaturalizing the familiar discourses of subjectivity which our culture promotes.

Analyzing the excesses of textuality, story, narration, and discourse intervenes in the cultural production of subjectivity, because it calls into question how and why narratives regulate meanings for us. Through its interruption of dominant suturing practices, such analysis opens up spaces for alternative and even new positions of intelligibility. The analysis we have demonstrated throughout this book can thus transform, through its fracturing of the text, not only the practices of reading and viewing but the subject of narrative as well.

# Notes

## 1 Theorizing language

1 For further discussion of "fiction" and "non-fiction" as functional categories of language use, see Smith 1978.

2 Although Saussure concentrated entirely on linguistics, his premises were developed (most notably in the 1950s by the anthropologist Claude Lévi-Strauss and the critic Roland Barthes) into a method of analyzing structures of all kinds, as well as sign systems. Often wrongly assumed to be indistinguishable from semiotics, this method of analysis became known as "structuralism" and was important to the study of narrative poetics (we shall discuss poetics in chapter 3). Many commentaries on structuralism include discussions of semiotics. Among the most helpful for further reading are: Scholes 1974, Culler 1975, and Hawkes 1977. Coward and Ellis 1977 offer a more critical account of Saussure's theory, as does Jameson 1972. Descombes 1980 locates semiotics along with structuralism in the philosophic tradition of French thought. Ducrot and Todorov 1979 provide informative entries on the key terms introduced by Saussure and widely used in both structuralist and semiotic analyses; an appendix summarizes the post-structuralist reexamination of the sign, a critique which we introduce in this chapter. Silverman 1983 offers excellent discussions of the sign, paradigm, and syntagm. Finally, the collection of essays in Blonsky 1985 displays the full range of contemporary semiotics as it examines verbal and non-verbal cultural signs.

3 V.N. Vološinov, assumed to be a pseudonym of the literary critic Mikhail Bakhtin, was one of the first to critique Saussure's emphasis

on the closed system of language (written in the 1920s, Vološinov's book was not translated from Russian into English until the 1970s). Two more recent critiques of Saussure, each discussing Vološinov's argument as a point of contrast, are Williams 1977 and Bennett 1979. See also Macdonell 1986 for a useful introduction to contemporary post-Saussurean arguments about language practices which move beyond Saussure's emphasis on language as a single closed system while still retaining the concepts of system and sign. We shall be taking up this issue of discourse at greater length in chapters 4, 5, and 6.

4  Saussure was not the only one to present a theory of the sign at the turn of the century. Writing and teaching at the same time as Saussure, the American philosopher Charles Sanders Peirce advanced a typology of signs which, in its attention to visual as well as verbal signs, has also informed contemporary semiotics. Peirce did not develop as complex a model for analyzing signification, nor did he stress the differential basis of signs, but he went further than Saussure in proposing that signs mediate meaning.

5  Derrida's critique of Saussure clearly does not reject the semiotic project; rather, as Christopher Norris points out, Derrida pushes Saussure's conclusions as far as they can go in order to analyze how they radically undermine the traditional premise of an extra-linguistic referentiality which supports the project (see Norris 1982: 24–32).


## 2   Analyzing textuality

1  A similar argument is also made by Kolodny 1985, Batsleer *et al.* 1985, and Scholes 1985.

2  Roman Jakobson, arguing that metaphor and metonymy are not simply tropes but fundamental binary operations of language, was the first to link metaphor to the paradigmatic axis of selection and metonymy to the syntagmatic axis of combination. See his essays on speech disorders (Jakobson 1971) and on poetry (Jakobson 1981).

3  For additional discussion of textuality in *Bleak House*, one which concentrates on the entire novel, see Connor 1985: 59–88.

4  Intertextuality should not be misunderstood as one text's providing the source for another or as a synonym for influence studies. More precisely, Kristeva states: "The term *inter-textuality* denotes this transposition of one (or several) sign system(s) into another; but since this term has often been understood in the banal sense of 'study of sources,' we prefer the term *transposition* because it specifies that the passage from one signifying system to another demands a new articulation . . . every signifying practice is a field of transpositions of

various signifying systems (an inter-textuality)" (Kristeva 1984: 59–60).

## 3 The structures of narrative: story

1 In narrative studies this distinction is more commonly put in terms of "story" and "discourse." For example, according to Seymour Chatman, "What is communicated is *story*, the formal content element of narrative; and it is communicated by *discourse*, the formal expression element" (Chatman 1978: 31). Since discourse is more than simply "formal expression," we prefer the term "narration."

Further, many narratologists claim that narrative is a three-part, not a two-part, relational system. Mieke Bal, for instance, follows the model of the Russian formalists, a group of critics writing in the Soviet Union during the 1920s whose studies of narrative in many ways laid the ground for contemporary poetics. She divides narrative into fabula, "a series of logically and chronologically related events"; story, "a fabula that is presented in a certain manner"; and text, "a finite, structured whole composed of language signs . . . in which an agent relates a narrative" (Bal 1985: 5). Not everyone studying narrative uses the same terms or defines the relations that comprise narrative in the same way. Wallace Martin surveys similarities between some of the most frequently used terms (Martin 1986: 108). We are using "story" and "narration" in the interest of clarity and simplicity.

2 Given limitations of length, we cannot attempt to display the variety of narrative texts classified by narrative poetics. Our objective in this chapter is, therefore, not to survey all possible narrative structures, nor to identify the structural unity of a given narrative through poetics, but to explain how story means as a signifying structure. For further reading in poetics, consult the bibliographies in Rimmon-Kenan 1983 and Martin 1986.

3 In "Introduction to the Structural Analysis of Narratives," Roland Barthes makes the same distinction but uses the term *nuclei* for "the hinge-points of narrative" and *catalysers* for those which "'fill in' the narrative space separating the hinge functions" (Barthes 1977:93).

4 This classification is Shlomith Rimmon-Kenan's, as based on her reading of Claude Bremond's analyses (Rimmon-Kenan 1983: 23); our definitions differ somewhat, however, for we are putting them in temporal terms, whereas she explains them strictly in terms of logical effects.

5 Our explanation is a simplified account of Greimas's "semiotic square" as set forth in *On Meaning* (Greimas 1987: 48–62).

6 The classifications derive from Vladimir Propp's analysis of such

stories in *Morphology of the Folk Tale* (Propp 1968), as modified by Greimas and others. Greimas distinguishes between the *actor*, an individual and recognizable character who occupies a functional position in relation to events, and the *actant*, that position examined as a class; the difference between actor and actant is analogous to that between a word and its grammatical classification. Greimas's point is to show that "actants and actors are not identical (one actant can be manifested by several actors and, conversely, one actor can at the same time represent several actants)" (Greimas 1987: 111). In the interests of clarity, we are using the term "actor" to designate the individual figure and "function" to designate the actantial role. See Bal 1985: 26–36 and Rimmon-Kenan 1983: 34–6 for additional discussions of Greimas's model.

7 Our discussion of the modern romance genre is indebted to the argument about the gendering of genres in Batsleer *et al.* 1985: 70–105.

## 4 The structures of narrative: narration

1 Benveniste's term "history" is sometimes translated as "story." It is therefore worth reiterating that he is *not* defining two fundamental levels of narrative (i.e. story and narration), but two levels of enunciation in the narration of a story.

## 5 Decoding texts: ideology, subjectivity, discourse

1 In his commentary on the symbolic code in *Sarrasine*, Barthes notes that the gendering of the characters at first appears consistent with a stable male/female antithesis according to their biological difference as men or women. So he initially poses the question of sexual difference in this way: male means "to be" the phallus, presumably because he has the penis as a symbol of power and therefore finds legitimation of his authority in nature, and female means "to have it," presumably because she biologically lacks what he has and can therefore only get access to it symbolically (Barthes 1974: 35). As Barthes examines this distribution of gender in the text, however, he then calls attention to the disparity between biological classification and symbolic roles. Showing how the text encodes one of the female characters "as the castrating woman endowed with all the hallucinatory attributes of the Father: power, fascination, instituting authority, terror, power to castrate," he concludes that "the symbolic field is not that of the biological sexes; it is that of castration: of *castrating/castrated, active/passive*" (36). As this more specific symbolic field organizes the antithesis of being/having the phallus, it clarifies

why that initial articulation of symbolic difference was "unsatisfactory" (35) – and ends up turning it around. For if the female's having the phallus threatens the male with castration – that is, with the emasculation or un-gendering of the male organ which results from her exposing that the phallus means only as a symbol and not in nature – then "male" does not mean being the phallus so much as *having* the plenitude which the phallus symbolizes, and "female" does not mean having the phallus so much as *being* the lack which having it symbolically relieves. We take up this issue again more fully in our discussion of the symbolic ordering of gendered subjectivities in chapter 6.

2 The essay, "Textual Analysis of a Tale of Poe," is reprinted, in different translations, in both Young 1981 and Blonsky 1985.

3 In a very influential early collection of essays, *Mythologies*, Barthes examines the transmission of ideology – which he called "cultural myths" – through the commutability of signs. See especially the conclusion "Myth Today" (Barthes 1972).

4 In introducing the term, our definition must necessarily simplify the scope of contemporary discussions about ideology. For additional introductory reading, see the entry on "ideology" in Williams 1977, Therborn 1980, McLellan 1986, and, for a summary of extensions and critiques of Althusser's theory, Macdonnell 1986. In addition to Raymond Williams, the most notable critics of ideology in Anglo-American literary studies are Terry Eagleton and Fredric Jameson, each of whom discusses the complex relation between history, ideology, and text. See Eagleton 1978 and Jameson 1981, as well as Dowling 1984 for a commentary on the latter. Finally, Thompson 1984 offers a wide-ranging critical survey of contemporary European theorists of ideology.

5 In chapter 6 we shall discuss why the subject must be understood as the effect of signification. For a more detailed explanation of the subject as a discursive production, see the sections entitled "Constructing the subject" and "Theorizing subjectivity" in Henriques *et al.* 1984.

6 In *The Birth of the Clinic*, Foucault examines the formation of medical discourse through the institution of medicine in the late eighteenth century (Foucault 1975).

7 For further reading on Foucault, see Dreyfus and Rabinow 1983.

## 6 The subject of narrative

1 More specifically, J. Laplanche and J.-B. Pontalis define *psychoanalysis* as follows:

Discipline founded by Freud, whose example we follow in considering it under three aspects:

  a. As a method of investigation which consists essentially in bringing out the unconscious meaning of the words, the actions and the products of the imagination (dreams, phantasies, delusions) of a particular subject. The method is founded mainly on the subject's free associations, which serve as the measuring-rod of the validity of the interpretation. Psycho-analytical interpretation can, however, be extended to human productions where no free associations are available.

  b. As a psychotherapeutic method based on this type of investigation and characterised by the controlled interpretation of resistance, transference and desire. It is in a related sense that the term "psycho-analysis" is used to mean a course of psycho-analytic treatment, as when one speaks of undergoing psycho-analysis (or analysis).

  c. As a group of psychological and psychopathological theories which are the systematic expression of the data provided by the psycho-analytic method of investigation and treatment. (Laplanche and Pontalis 1973: 367–8)

Our use of psychoanalytic theory may seem universal, all the more so because the psychological is easily essentialized as human nature. But if, as psychoanalysis itself argues, subjectivity is produced by signifying activities which are historically specific and often culturally unconscious, so are theories of subjectivity, and psychoanalysis is no exception.

2 For additional discussion of the *fort/da* game, see Silverman 1983: 167–74 and Thom 1981: 32–4; the latter also offers a more detailed explanation than we are providing of the Lacanian tenet that the unconscious is structured like a language. For further reading on Lacan's theories, see Wilden 1981, Lemaire 1977, and Rose 1986.

3 Put in another, more provocative way: "Desire does not lack anything; it does not lack its object. It is, rather, the *subject* that is missing in desire, or desire that lacks a fixed subject; there is no fixed subject unless there is repression. Desire and its object are one and the same thing" (Deleuze and Guattari 1977: 26).

4 The *fort/da* game, in other words, represents a drive as desire through a symbol of negation. "The moment of the throwing out of the toy has a double structure: it affirms the presence that it constructs at the moment of constructing it, but this affirmation is itself denegated, such that the affirmation 'it is she' or 'it is my mother' nestles within the denegation 'it isn't she,' 'it isn't my mother'" (Thom 1981: 34).

5 The phallus, especially as symbolized for the subject through Oedi-

palization, reinstates for each individual the phallocentrism of western culture, which defines the female negationally as "not male." The controversial status of the phallus, which is easily naturalized as a question of biology, therefore arises from its cultural importance. For a full account of Oedipalization in Lacanian terms, see "The Phallic Phase and the Subjective Import of the Castration Complex" (Lacan and the *école freudienne* 1982: 99–122). For a critique of the universalized status of Oedipalization in psychoanalysis, see Deleuze and Guattari 1977.

Psychoanalytic feminism attests to the importance of the phallus in determining gender identity, while rejecting Freud's phallocentrism. Juliet Mitchell and Jacqueline Rose mediate the relation of Lacanian psychoanalysis and feminism in their introductions to *Feminine Sexuality* (Lacan and the *école freudienne* 1982). Much contemporary French feminist theory does not take so charitable a stand; for different critiques of Lacan, and for theories of the feminine as an alternative cultural space, see Cixous and Clément 1986, Irigaray 1985a and 1985b, and Kristeva 1986. See also the essays in Marks and de Courtivron 1981, and, for a bibliography, see Moi 1985.

6 The essays in De Lauretis and Heath 1980 indicate the range of critical discussion about the cinematic apparatus.

# References

Althusser, Louis (1971) *Lenin and Philosophy and Other Essays*, trans. Ben Brewster, New York: Monthly Review Press. Essays first published in French 1964–70.

—— (1977) *For Marx*, trans. Ben Brewster, London: New Left Books. First published in French in 1965.

Armstrong, Nancy (1987) *Desire and Domestic Fiction*, New York: Oxford University Press.

Austen, Jane (1966) *Pride and Prejudice*, ed. Donald J. Gray, New York: Norton. First published in 1813.

Bal, Mieke (1985) *Narratology: Introduction to the Theory of Narrative*, 2nd rev. edn, trans. Christine van Boheemen, Toronto: University of Toronto Press. First published in Dutch in 1980.

Barthes, Roland (1972) *Mythologies*, selected and trans. Annette Lavers, New York: Hill & Wang. First published in French in 1957.

—— (1974) *S/Z*, trans. Richard Miller, New York: Hill & Wang. First published in French in 1970.

—— (1977) *Image–Music–Text*, trans. Stephen Heath, New York: Hill & Wang. Essays first published in French 1961–71.

—— (1981) "Theory of the Text," trans. Ian McLeod, in Robert Young (ed.), *Untying the Text: A Post-Structuralist Reader*, Boston, Mass.: Routledge & Kegan Paul, 31–47. First published in French in 1973.

Batsleer, Janet, Davies, Tony, O'Rourke, Rebecca, and Weedon, Chris (1985) *Rewriting English*, London: Methuen.

Baudry, Jean-Louis (1986) "Ideological Effects of the Basic Cinematographic Apparatus," trans. Alan Williams, in Philip Rosen (ed.), *Narrative, Apparatus, Ideology: A Film Theory Reader*, New York:

Columbia University Press, 286–98. First published in French in 1970.

Belsey, Catherine (1980) *Critical Practice*, London: Methuen.

Bennett, Tony (1979) *Formalism and Marxism*, London: Methuen.

Benveniste, Emile (1971) *Problems in General Linguistics*, trans. Mary Elizabeth Meek, Coral Gables, Fla.: University of Miami Press. First published in French in 1966.

Blonsky, Marshall (ed.) (1985) *On Signs*, Baltimore: Johns Hopkins University Press.

Brontë, Charlotte (1971) *Jane Eyre*, ed. Richard J. Dunn, New York: Norton. First published in 1847.

Calvino, Italo (1981) *If on a winter's night a traveler*, trans. William Weaver, New York: Harcourt Brace Jovanovich. First published in Italian in 1979.

Carroll, Lewis (1960) *Alice's Adventures in Wonderland*, New York: New American Library. First published in 1865.

Chatman, Seymour (1978) *Story and Discourse: Narrative Structure in Fiction and Film*, Ithaca, NY: Cornell University Press.

Cixous, Hélène, and Clément, Catherine (1986) *The Newly Born Woman*, trans. Betsy Wing, Minneapolis: University of Minnesota Press. First published in French in 1975.

Cohn, Dorrit (1978) *Transparent Minds: Narrative Modes for Presenting Consciousness in Fiction*, Princeton, NJ: Princeton University Press.

Connor, Steven (1985) *Charles Dickens*, Oxford: Basil Blackwell.

Conrad, Joseph (1968) *Lord Jim*, ed. Thomas Moser, New York: Norton. First published in 1900.

Coward, Rosalind (1985) *Female Desires: How They Are Sought, Bought, and Packaged*, New York: Grove Press.

—— and Ellis, John (1977) *Language and Materialism: Developments in Semiology and the Theory of the Subject*, London: Routledge & Kegan Paul.

Culler, Jonathan (1975) *Structuralist Poetics: Structuralism, Linguistics, and the Study of Literature*, Ithaca, NY: Cornell University Press.

Dailey, Janet (1981) *The Hostage Bride*, New York: Pocket Books.

Dayan, Daniel (1976) "The Tutor-Code of Classical Cinema," in Bill Nichols (ed.), *Movies and Methods*, Berkeley: University of California Press, 438–51. First published in 1974.

De Lauretis, Teresa, and Heath, Stephen (eds) (1980) *The Cinematic Apparatus*, New York: St Martin's Press.

Deleuze, Gilles, and Guattari, Félix (1977) *Anti-Oedipus: Capitalism and Schizophrenia*, trans. Robert Hurley, Mark Seem, and Helen R. Lane, Minneapolis: University of Minnesota Press. First published in French in 1972.

Derrida, Jacques (1976) *Of Grammatology*, trans. Gayatri Chakravorty Spivak, Baltimore: Johns Hopkins University Press. First published in French in 1967.

—— (1978) *Writing and Difference*, trans. Alan Bass, Chicago: University of Chicago Press. First published in French in 1967.

Descombes, Vincent (1980) *Modern French Philosophy*, trans. L. Scott-Fox and J.M. Harding, Cambridge: Cambridge University Press. First published in French in 1979.

Dickens, Charles (1965) *Great Expectations*, ed. Angus Calder, Harmondsworth: Penguin. First published in 1861.

—— (1977) *Bleak House*, ed. George Ford and Sylvère Monad, New York: Norton. First published in 1853.

Doane, Mary Ann (1987) *The Desire to Desire: The Woman's Film of the 1940s*, Bloomington: Indiana University Press.

Dowling, William C. (1984) *Jameson, Althusser, Marx: An Introduction to The Political Unconscious*, Ithaca, NY: Cornell University Press.

Dreyfus, Hubert L., and Rabinow, Paul (1983) *Michel Foucault: Beyond Structuralism and Hermeneutics*, 2nd rev. edn, Chicago: University of Chicago Press.

Ducrot, Oswald, and Todorov, Tzvetan (1979) *Encyclopedic Dictionary of the Sciences of Language*, trans. Catherine Porter, Baltimore: Johns Hopkins University Press. First published in French in 1972.

Eagleton, Terry (1978) *Criticism and Ideology: A Study in Marxist Literary Theory*, London: Verso. First published in 1976.

—— (1983) *Literary Theory: An Introduction*, Minneapolis: University of Minnesota Press.

Faulkner, William (1931) *Sanctuary*, New York: Random House.

Forster, E.M. (1927) *Aspects of the Novel*, New York: Harcourt, Brace & World.

Foucault, Michel (1972) *The Archaeology of Knowledge*, trans. A.M. Sheridan Smith, New York: Pantheon. First published in French in 1969.

—— (1975) *The Birth of the Clinic: An Archaeology of Medical Perception*, trans. A.M. Sheridan Smith, New York: Vintage Books. First published in French in 1963.

—— (1977) *Language, Counter-Memory, Practice: Selected Essays and Interviews*, ed. Donald F. Bouchard, trans. Donald F. Bouchard and Sherry Simon, Ithaca, NY: Cornell University Press. Essays first published in French 1962–71.

—— (1983) "The Subject and Power," in Hubert L. Dreyfus and Paul Rabinow, *Michel Foucault: Beyond Structuralism and Hermeneutics*, 2nd rev. edn, Chicago: University of Chicago Press, 208–26.

Fowler, Roger (1977) *Linguistics and the Novel*, London: Methuen.

Freud, Sigmund (1961) *Beyond the Pleasure Principle*, trans. and ed.

James Strachey, New York: Norton. First published in German in 1920.

—— (1977) *Introductory Lectures on Psychoanalysis*, trans. and ed. James Strachey, New York: Norton. First published in German 1916–17.

Genette, Gérard (1980) *Narrative Discourse: An Essay in Method*, trans. Jane E. Lewin, Ithaca, NY: Cornell University Press. First published in French as *Figures III* in 1972.

Green, Henry (1978) *Three Novels: Loving, Living, and Party Going*, Harmondsworth: Penguin. *Party Going* first published in 1939.

Greene, Graham (1977) *Brighton Rock*, Harmondsworth: Penguin. First published in 1938.

Greimas, A.J. (1987) *On Meaning: Selected Writings in Semiotic Theory*, trans. Paul J. Perron and Frank H. Collins, Minneapolis: University of Minnesota Press. First published in French 1970–83.

Hardy, Thomas (1964) *Tess of the d'Urbervilles*, New York: New American Library. First published in 1891.

Hawkes, Terence (1977) *Structuralism and Semiotics*, London: Methuen; Berkeley: University of California Press.

Heath, Stephen (1981) *Questions of Cinema*, Bloomington: Indiana University Press.

Hemingway, Ernest (1926) *The Sun Also Rises*, New York: Charles Scribner's Sons.

Henriques, Julian, Hollway, Wendy, Urwin, Cathy, Venn, Couze, and Walkerdine, Valerie (1984) *Changing the Subject: Psychology, Social Regulation and Subjectivity*, London: Methuen.

Irigaray, Luce (1985a) *This Sex Which Is Not One*, trans. Catherine Porter, Ithaca, NY: Cornell University Press. First published in French in 1977.

—— (1985b) *Speculum of the Other Woman*, trans. Gillian C. Gill, Ithaca, NY: Cornell University Press. First published in French in 1974.

Jakobson, Roman (1971) "Two Aspects of Language and Two Types of Aphasic Disturbances," in *Selected Writings*, vol. 2: *Word and Language*, The Hague: Mouton, 239–59. First published in 1956.

—— (1981) "Linguistics and Poetics," in *Selected Writings*, vol. 3: *Grammar of Poetry and Poetry of Grammar*, The Hague: Mouton. First published in 1960.

Jameson, Fredric (1972) *The Prison House of Language: A Critical Account of Structuralism and Russian Formalism*, Princeton, NJ: Princeton University Press.

—— (1981) *The Political Unconscious: Narrative as a Socially Symbolic Act*, Ithaca, NY: Cornell University Press.

Johnson, Richard (1986–7) "What is Cultural Studies Anyway?," *Social Text*, 16, 1: 38–80.

Joyce, James (1962) *Dubliners*, New York: Viking. First published in 1916.

—— (1976) *A Portrait of the Artist as a Young Man*, Harmondsworth: Penguin. First published in 1916.

Kaplan, Cora (1985) "Pandora's Box: Subjectivity, Class and Sexuality in Socialist Feminist Criticism," in Gayle Greene and Coppélia Kahn (eds), *Making a Difference: Feminist Literary Criticism*, London: Methuen, 146–76.

Kolodny, Annette (1985) "Dancing through the Minefield: Some Observations on the Theory, Practice, and Politics of a Feminist Literary Criticism," in Elaine Showalter (ed.), *The New Feminist Criticism: Essays on Women, Literature, Theory*, New York: Pantheon. First published in 1980.

Kristeva, Julia (1980) *Desire in Language: A Semiotic Approach to Literature and Art*, ed. Leon S. Roudiez, trans. Thomas Gora, Alice Jardine, Leon S. Roudiez, New York: Columbia University Press. First published in French in 1969 and 1977.

—— (1984) *Revolution in Poetic Language*, trans. Margaret Waller, New York: Columbia University Press. First published in French in 1974.

—— (1986) *The Kristeva Reader*, ed. Toril Moi, New York: Columbia University Press.

Kuhn, Annette (1982) *Women's Pictures: Feminism and Cinema*, London: Routledge & Kegan Paul.

Lacan, Jacques (1977) *Ecrits: A Selection*, trans. Alan Sheridan, New York: Norton. Essays first published in French 1948–60.

—— (1978) *The Four Fundamental Concepts of Psycho-Analysis*, ed. Jacques-Alain Miller, trans. Alan Sheridan, New York: Norton. First published in French in 1973.

—— and the *école freudienne* (1982) *Feminine Sexuality*, ed. Juliet Mitchell and Jacqueline Rose, trans. Jacqueline Rose, New York: Norton. First published in French 1966–75; editors' introductions 1982.

Lanser, Susan Sniader (1981) *The Narrative Act: Point of View in Prose Fiction*, Princeton, NJ: Princeton University Press.

Laplanche, J., and Pontalis, J.-B. (1973) *The Language of Psycho-Analysis*, trans. Donald Nicholson-Smith, New York: Norton. First published in French in 1967.

Lawrence, D.H. (1976a) *Sons and Lovers*, Harmondsworth: Penguin. First published in 1913.

—— (1976b) *Women in Love*, Harmondsworth: Penguin. First published in 1920.

Lemaire, Anika (1977) *Jacques Lacan*, trans. David Macey, London: Routledge & Kegan Paul. First published in French in 1970.

MacCabe, Colin (1985) *Tracking the Signifier: Theoretical Essays: Film, Linguistics, Literature*, Minneapolis: University of Minnesota Press.

Macdonell, Diane (1986) *Theories of Discourse: An Introduction*, Oxford: Basil Blackwell.

McLellan, David (1986) *Ideology*, Minneapolis: University of Minnesota Press.

Marks, Elaine, and de Courtivron, Isabelle (1981) *New French Feminisms*, New York: Schocken Books.

Martin, Wallace (1986) *Recent Theories of Narrative*, Ithaca, NY: Cornell University Press.

Maugham, W. Somerset (1951) "The Letter," in *Complete Short Stories*, vol. 1: *East and West*, Garden City, NY: Doubleday. First published in 1924.

Metz, Christian (1982) *The Imaginary Signifier: Psychoanalysis and the Cinema*, trans. Celia Britton, Annwyl Williams, Ben Brewster, and Alfred Guzzetti, Bloomington: Indiana University Press. First published in French in 1977.

Miller, D.A. (1981) *Narrative and its Discontents: Problems of Closure in the Traditional Novel*, Princeton, NJ: Princeton University Press.

Miller, Jacques-Alain (1977–8) "Suture (elements of the logic of the signifier)," *Screen*, 18, 4:24–34.

Moi, Toril (1985) *Sexual/Textual Politics: Feminist Literary Theory*, London: Methuen.

Monaco, James (1981) *How to Read a Film: The Art, Technology, Language, History, and Theory of Film and Media*, rev. edn, New York: Oxford University Press.

Murdoch, Iris (1976) *Bruno's Dream*, New York: Penguin. First published in 1969.

Norris, Christopher (1982) *Deconstruction: Theory and Practice*, London: Methuen.

Oudart, Jean-Pierre (1977–8) "Cinema and Suture," *Screen*, 18, 4: 35–47.

Peirce, Charles Sanders (1955) "Logic as Semiotic: The Theory of Signs," in *Philosophical Writings of Peirce*, ed. Justus Buchler, New York: Dover.

Propp, Vladimir (1968) *Morphology of the Folk Tale*, 2nd rev. edn, ed. Louis A. Wagner, trans. Laurence Scott, Austin: University of Texas Press. First published in Russian in 1928.

Puig, Manuel (1981) *Heartbreak Tango: A Serial*, trans. Suzanne Jill Levine, New York: Vintage. First published in Spanish in 1969.

Rabine, Leslie W. (1985) "Romance in the Age of Electronics: Harlequin Enterprise," in Judith Newton and Deborah Rosenfelt (eds), *Feminist Criticism and Social Change*, New York: Methuen, 249–67.

Rimmon-Kenan, Shlomith (1983) *Narrative Fiction: Contemporary Poetics*, London: Methuen.

Rose, Jacqueline (1986) *Sexuality in the Field of Vision*, London: Verso.

Saussure, Ferdinand de (1966) *Course in General Linguistics*, trans. Wade Baskin, New York: McGraw-Hill. First published in French in 1915.

Scholes, Robert (1974) *Structuralism in Literature: An Introduction*, New Haven, Conn.: Yale University Press.

—— (1985) *Textual Power: Literary Theory and the Teaching of English*, New Haven, Conn.: Yale University Press.

Sebeok, Thomas A. (1985) "Pandora's Box: How and Why to Communicate 10,000 Years into the Future," in Marshall Blonsky (ed.), *On Signs*, Baltimore: Johns Hopkins University Press, 448–66.

Silverman, Kaja (1983) *The Subject of Semiotics*, New York: Oxford University Press.

Smith, Barbara Herrnstein (1978) *On the Margins of Discourse: The Relation of Literature to Language*, Chicago: University of Chicago Press.

Stoker, Bram (1965) *Dracula*, New York: New American Library. First published in 1897.

Therborn, Gören (1980) *The Ideology of Power and the Power of Ideology*, London: Verso.

Thom, Martin (1981) "The Unconscious Structured as a Language," in Colin MacCabe (ed.), *The Talking Cure: Essays in Psychoanalysis and Language*, New York: St Martin's Press, 1–44.

Thomas, Lewis (1983) *The Youngest Science: Notes of a Medicine-Watcher*, New York: Bantam.

Thompson, John B. (1984) *Studies in the Theory of Ideology*, Berkeley: University of California Press.

Todorov, Tzvetan (1977) *The Poetics of Prose*, trans. Richard Howard, Ithaca, NY: Cornell University Press. First published in French in 1971.

—— (1981) *Introduction to Poetics*, trans. Richard Howard, Minneapolis: University of Minnesota Press. First published in French in 1968 and 1973.

Vološinov, V.N. (1986) *Marxism and the Philosophy of Language*, trans. Ladislav Matejka and I.R. Titunik, Cambridge, Mass.: Harvard University Press. First published in Russian in 1929.

Weeks, Jeffrey (1986) *Sexuality*, London: Tavistock/Ellis Horwood.

Wilden, Anthony (1981) *Speech and Language in Psychoanalysis*, Baltimore: Johns Hopkins University Press. First published in 1968 as *The Language of the Self*.

Williams, Raymond (1977) *Marxism and Literature*, Oxford: Oxford University Press.

—— (1983) *Keywords: A Vocabulary of Culture and Society*, rev. edn, New York: Oxford University Press.

Williamson, Judith (1978) *Decoding Advertisements: Ideology and Meaning in Advertising*, London: Marion Boyars.

Woolf, Virginia (1927) *To the Lighthouse*, New York: Harcourt Brace & World.

Young, Robert (ed.) (1981) *Untying the Text: A Post-Structuralist Reader*, Boston, Mass.: Routledge & Kegan Paul.

# Index of terms

achrony 85
anachrony 84
analepsis 85

binary opposition 37

closure 65
code 114
consonant psycho-narration 100
convention 3

diachronic 16
diegesis 88
discourse 10, 93, 139
dissonant psycho-narration 100

ellipsis 89
embedded events 57
enchained events 57
event 53–4
external focalization 96

fiction 2
focalization 95
focalized 95
focalizer 95
figural (internal) focalization 96
free indirect discourse 101

genre 77

helper function 69
hermeneutic code 119
history (historical narration) 93
homology 39

ideology 133
imaginary register 157
interior monologue 99
intertextuality 50
iterative event 86

joined events 58

kernel event 54

langue 10

macrostructure 59
metaphor 27
metonymy 28
microstructure 59
mimesis 88

narrated dialogue 98
narrated monologue 99
narrated subject 108

narrating agency 89
narrating subject 108
narration 53
narrative 1
narratology 53
narrator 90

object function 69
opponent function 69

paradigm 12
paradigmatic binary opposition 37
paradigmatic metaphor 34
paradigmatic metonymy 35–6
paraphrased dialogue 98
parole 10
pause 88
poetics 53
proairetic code 119
prolepsis 85
pseudo-iterative event 86
psycho-narration 100

quoted dialogue 97
quoted monologue 99

receiver function 69
reference code 120
referent 11
referent system 115
repeated event 86

satellite event 54
scene 88

semic code 119
semiotics 10
sender function 69
sequence 54
sign 10
signified 10
signifier 10
singular event 86
slow-down 88
speaking subject 105
spoken subject 105
story 53
stream of consciousness 99
subject function 69
subject of narration 108
subject of speech 105
summary 87
suture 162
symbolic code 120
symbolic register 158–9
synchronic 16
syntagm 14
syntagmatic binary opposition 37
syntagmatic metaphor 34
syntagmatic metonymy 34

temporal duration 87
temporal frequency 85–6
temporal order 84
text 25–6
textuality 21
trait 72

work 25

# Index

*Alice's Adventures in Wonderland*
(Lewis Carroll) 5–9, 11–18
*passim*, 58
Althusser, Louis 133, 136, 138
Armstrong, Nancy 80–1, 145

Bakhtin, Mikhail, *see* V. N.
Vološinov
Bal, Mieke 108, 178n.1, 179n.6
Barthes, Roland 176n.2, 178n.3,
180n.3; *S/Z*: codes 118–20,
132–3: hermeneutic 123–4;
proairetic 120–1; reference
127–31; semic 121–3;
symbolic 124–7, 179–90n.1;
text v. work 25–6; *see also* codes
Benveniste, Emile 92–3, 104–5,
179n.1
binary opposition 37–8;
paradigmatic 43–4, 46–7; and
sexual difference 159–61; in
the symbolic code 120, 124–7;
syntagmatic 43; in *Bleak House*
46–9, 50, 113; in *Dracula*
126–7; in the *fort/da* game
(Freud) 158; in "In a Station
of the Metro" 20, 30; in *The
Letter* 37–40; in *Pride and
Prejudice* 43, 44, 67–8, 76, 117;

in *The Youngest Science* 32
*Bleak House* (Charles Dickens) 2,
44–51, 91, 113–14, 121, 129,
130, 174, 177n.3
*Brighton Rock* (Graham Greene)
129–30
*Bruno's Dream* (Iris Murdoch) 85

*Cathy* 55–8, 59, 78, 88, 123
character 50, 52, 90–2, 95–6,
98–102, 106–11 *passim*, 121–3,
123, 165; functions 69–72, 76,
77, 79, 83, 117, 178–9n.6;
traits 72–6, 78–9, 97, 108, 119,
121–3, 134, 153
Chatman, Seymour 72, 75,
178n.1
closure 26, 49–50, 64–8, 78–82
*passim*, 119, 124, 125, 147–8,
151, 153, 169, 171, 173
codes 3–5, 114–15, 117–19,
132–3, 135, 143, 172–3;
hermeneutic 119, 123–4, 125,
127, 143, 147, 151, 173;
proairetic 119, 120–1, 122,
123, 131, 134, 143, 173;
reference 115–16, 118, 120,
124, 127–31, 132, 140, 143–4,
173, 180n.2; semic 119, 121–3,

codes – *cont.*
123, 125, 126, 131, 132, 137,
143, 153, 172; symbolic 120,
124–7, 131, 132, 135, 137, 143,
147, 153, 160, 172, 179–80n.1;
in Woolrich clothing
advertisement 115–17, 129,
134; *see also* intertextuality
Cohn, Dorrit 99
Connor, Steven 177n.3
convention 3–4, 13, 18, 22–4, 27,
50, 51, 77, 113
Coward, Rosalind 79
Coward, Rosalind and Ellis,
John 137, 176n.2
Culler, Jonathan 22, 26, 27–8

Dayan, Daniel 165
Deleuze, Gilles and Guattari,
Félix 181n.3, 182n.5
Derrida, Jacques 19–20, 37–8,
177n.5
desire 68, 70, 71–2, 76, 79, 80,
81, 82, 137, 152, 153, 154–6,
159, 160, 162, 168, 171, 172,
181n.3
diegesis 88, 131, 137, 163, 164,
165, 167, 172
discourse 16, 20, 37–8, 51, 83,
90, 135, 177n.3, 178n.1; as
articulation and practice 10,
14, 15, 17–19, 22, 30, 139–48,
168, 171, 173–4, 176–7n.3,
180n.6; as site of subjectivity
104–12, 136–9, 149, 152–3,
156, 161–2, 163, 170–1,
180n.5; versus history in
narration 93–4, 104, 179n.1; in
*Jane Eyre* 109–12, 142–8, 171
Doane, Mary Ann 160
*Dracula* (Bram Stoker) 126–7

Eagleton, Terry 23–4, 129,
180n.4

"Eveline" (James Joyce) 122–3,
130
event 53–4, 66–8, 82, 83, 117,
169; and characters 69–72,
75–6, 79; combination 57–8,
61–4, 64–5; kernel and
satellite 54–7, 59, 59–64,
64–5, 75–6, 84, 86, 87, 120,
121; sequence 54, 58–64,
64–6, 77, 120, 122, 123–4; *see
also* closure; codes; narration;
temporality

fiction 2, 3
focalization 50, 52, 83, 95, 96,
98–9, 100, 102, 108, 131, 137,
165; external 95–9, 108;
figural (internal) 96–8, 104,
106, 109, 110, 131; in *Jane Eyre*
109–12, 171; in *The Letter*
165–6, 167–8; in "The Letter"
96–7, 131; in *Pride and Prejudice*
102–3, 108; *see also* narration;
suture
Forster, E. M. 58
*fort/da* game (Freud) 155–6,
157–9, 161, 166, 181n.2,
181n.4
Foucault, Michel 139–42,
180n.6, 180n.7
Freud, Sigmund 154–6, 157–8,
161, 182n.5

gender, *see* sexual difference
Genette, Gérard 84, 86, 96
genre 77–82, 153, 179n.7
*Great Expectations* (Charles
Dickens) 41, 42, 43–4
Greimas, A. J. 67–8, 178n.5,
178–9n.6

*Heartbreak Tango* (Manuel Puig)
90–1, 93, 94, 128, 129
Heath, Stephen 163, 165

historical narration, *see* discourse
history 51, 80–2, 130, 131,
    134–5, 140, 142, 145–6, 173
*Hostage Bride, The* (Janet Dailey)
    73, 81–2

identification (reader, viewer)
    105–8 *passim*, 137–8, 150,
    150–3, 157–8, 160, 162–72
ideology 77–82, 114, 133–9, 141,
    142, 144–8, 166–7, 173–4,
    180n.3, 180n.4
*If on a winter's night a traveler*
    (Italo Calvino) 92, 150–3, 154,
    170–1
imaginary register 133–4, 157–8,
    159, 163–6, 168, 169, 170–1
"In a Station of the Metro"
    (Ezra Pound) 26–30
intertextuality 50–1, 113, 118,
    122, 129, 130, 166–7, 173,
    177–8n.4

Jakobson, Roman 177n.2
Jameson, Fredric 180n.4
*Jane Eyre* (Charlotte Brontë):
    codes 143–4; discourses of
    142–8, 171, 173, 174; genre 78,
    80–1; metaphor 41, 44;
    narration of 90, 91, 109–12,
    171
Johnson, Richard 77–8

Kaplan, Cora 146
Kristeva, Julia 51, 117–18n.4

Lacan, Jacques 125, 156–62,
    181n.2, 181n.5
*Lady in the Lake* (dir. Robert
    Montgomery) 164
language: as discourse (*parole*)
    16, 17–20, 139, 176–7n.3; of
    driving 3–5, 17–18; paradigms
    12–14, 17; as sign system

(*langue*) 10–15, 16, 17, 18, 20;
    syntagms 14–15, 17; *Alice's
    Adventures in Wonderland* 5–9,
    11–18 *passim*; *see also* binary
    opposition; codes; discourse;
    metaphor and metonymy;
    pronouns; subjectivity;
    textuality
Laplanche, J. and Pontalis, J.-B.
    180–1n.1
*Letter, The* (dir. William Wyler):
    codes 123; narration 86; story
    66–7, 70–2; suture 165–9,
    172–3; textuality 34–40
"Letter, The" (W. Somerset
    Maugham) 96–7, 131, 137,
    138
literary competence 22–8, 53,
    77–8, 117, 131, 174
*Lord Jim* (Joseph Conrad) 85, 86

MacCabe, Colin 161
metaphor and metonymy 22,
    27–50, 54, 65, 66, 73–4, 117,
    124–5, 135, 152, 165, 167, 168,
    177n.2
Metz, Christian 33–4, 37, 163
Miller, D. A. 65
Miller, Jacques-Alain 162
Mitchell, Juliet 182n.5

narration 1–2, 49, 53, 82, 83–4,
    88, 89–94, 102–4, 106–7, 113,
    123, 131, 137, 142, 172,
    178n.1, 179n.1; of dialogue
    97–8; division of subjectivity
    in 104–7, 107–12, 143–4,
    150–3; free indirect discourse
    101–2, 104; interior
    monologue 99, 106; narrated
    monologue 99–100, 101, 102,
    104; narrating agency 89–92,
    93, 94, 95; psycho-narration
    99, 100–1, 102, 103, 104;

narration – *cont.*
  quoted monologue 99, 102,
  106, 110, 171; *see also*
  focalization; suture;
  temporality
Norris, Christopher 177n.5

Oudart, Jean-Pierre 165, 169

paradigm 12–14, 21, 24, 33, 44,
  72–5 *passim*, 77, 80, 92, 103,
  118, 126, 149, 157, 161, 167,
  169, 176n.2, 177n.2; binary
  opposition 37, 43–4, 46–7;
  metaphor 34, 41, 47, 74;
  metonymy 35–6, 42–3, 45, 46,
  47, 73–4; story 54, 64–8, 69,
  70, 76, 78, 80, 81, 82, 102, 113,
  117, 125
*Party Going* (Henry Green) 41
Peirce, Charles S. 19, 177n.4
poetics 53, 176n.2, 178n.2
*Portrait of the Artist as a Young
  Man, A* (James Joyce) 41,
  99–100, 101–2
*Pride and Prejudice* (Jane Austen):
  binary opposition 43, 44;
  character traits 73–6, 121;
  codes 120–1, 121, 123, 125,
  129; genre 78–82; narration
  83, 84, 86, 88, 91, 100–1,
  102–3, 108, 108–9; story
  paradigm 65, 67–8, 76, 80,
  117, 125; story syntagm
  59–64, 65, 76, 120–1, 123
pronouns 8–9, 15–16, 90–2, 97,
  104–5, 109, 110, 136–8,
  150–3, 170–1
Propp, Vladimir 178–9
psychoanalysis 149, 154–62,
  180–1n.1, 181–2n.5

Rabine, Leslie 81
referent 3, 7, 20, 104–6, 107, 108,
  161; *see also* codes

Rimmon-Kenan, Shlomith 59,
  73, 179n.6
Rose, Jacqueline 160, 182n.5

*Sanctuary* (William Faulkner) 40,
  42
Saussure, Ferdinand de 9–20,
  176n.2, 176–7n.3, 177n.4,
  177n.5
*Secret Agent, The* (Joseph Conrad)
  88
semiotics 10, 11, 24, 25, 79, 81,
  176n.2, 177n.4; *see also* sign
sexual difference 33–40, 72, 73,
  75, 76, 78–82, 97, 122, 124–7,
  129, 130, 131, 134, 143–8
  *passim*, 151–3, 148–61, 167–74
  *passim*, 179–80n.1, 181–2n.5
sign 10–20, 21, 33, 52, 67–8,
  79–80, 113, 124, 132, 135, 138,
  158, 161, 166, 176n.2, 177n.3,
  180n.3; commutability of 19,
  20, 25–9, 37–9, 44–51, 108,
  113–14, 117, 119, 121–3, 126,
  130, 132, 180n.3;
  differentiation of 11, 16, 21,
  37–9, 107; driving as sign
  system 3–5, 17–18;
  paradigmatic relations 12–14,
  21, 34–6, 41–4, 65; relation of
  signifier and signified 10–11,
  16, 21, 22, 79, 105, 107–8, 131,
  135, 166; syntagmatic
  relations 14–15, 21, 34, 34–5,
  37, 40–4, 105, 136; *see also*
  codes; subjectivity; suture
Silverman, Kaja 105, 106, 165,
  166, 169, 176n.2, 181n.2
*Sons and Lovers* (D. H. Lawrence)
  86–7
subject: narrated 107–12, 152–3,
  162, 164, 166, 170, 171;
  narrating 107–12, 163, 165,
  170, 171; speaking 105–8, 149,

156, 161; spoken 105–7; of
events 69–72, 76, 79, 81, 136,
142, 150–3, 170; of narration
107–12, 142, 144, 150, 164,
165, 170, 171; of speech 105–8,
142, 156
subjectivity 84, 93, 94, 104, 112,
149, 153, 174, 180n.5;
focalization of 98–9, 100, 137;
and ideology 78, 79–80,
135–9, 140–1, 143–8, 149,
171, 173; psychoanalytic
model of 149, 154–72, 181n.1
*Sun Also Rises, The* (Ernest
Hemingway) 40–1
suture 162–75
symbolic register 125–6, 158–62,
166–9, 170–1, 172, 179–80n.1,
181n.4, 181–2n.5
syntagm 14–15, 17, 21, 33, 44,
71, 74–5, 102, 103, 149, 157,
161, 163, 166, 169, 176n.2,
177n.2; binary opposition 37,
43, 46–7; metaphor 34–5,
40–1, 48; metonymy 34–5,
41–2, 45; story 54, 54–64,
64–79 *passim*, 82, 87, 113

temporality 83, 109, 163;

duration 87–9, 93, 100, 120;
frequency 85–7, 89, 93; order
52, 84–7, 89, 93, 99; story
57–9, 120, 124
*Tess of the d'Urbervilles* (Thomas
Hardy) 41–2, 44
textuality 21, 24–6, 28–51, 65,
97, 107, 112, 113, 118, 157,
161, 173, 177; *see also*
intertextuality; codes
Thom, Martin 181n.2, 181n.4
*To the Lighthouse* (Virginia Woolf)
97–8
Todorov, Tzvetan 54, 58

Vološinov, V. N. 16, 176–7n.3

Williams, Raymond 180n.4
Williamson, Judith 115, 132, 135
*Women in Love* (D. H. Lawrence)
40, 43
Woolrich clothing advertisement
115–17, 129, 132, 134–5, 137,
138, 140

Young, Robert 21, 26
*Youngest Science, The* (Lewis
Thomas) 30–3